MAKING BEAD & WIRE JEWELRY

MAKING
BEAD & WIRE
JEWELRY

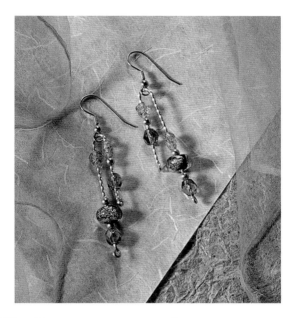

Simple Techniques, Stunning Designs

DAWN CUSICK

LARK BOOKS
A Division of Sterling Publishing Co., Inc.
New York

Photo Styling and Design: CELIA NARANJO
Photography: DWAYNE SHELL
Illustrations: HANNES CHAREN
Production and Layout: DAWN CUSICK
Editorial Assistance: HEATHER SMITH, CATHARINE SUTHERLAND
Production Assistance: HANNES CHAREN, M.E. KIRBY
Proofreading: JULIE BROWN

Published by Lark Books, a division of
Sterling Publishing Co., Inc.
387 Park Avenue South, New York, N.Y. 10016

© 2000, Lark Books

Every effort has been made to ensure that all the information in this book is accurate. However, due to differing conditions, tools, and individual skills, the publisher cannot be responsible for any injuries, losses, and other damages that may result from the use of the information in this book.

ISBN 978-1-57990-148-6

CONTENTS

INTRODUCTION

The concept of trends in jewelry styles is nothing new. For thousands of years humans have adorned themselves with jewelry, and for most of those years the styles were fairly consistent within societies. In the Viking culture, for example, leaders wore gold and silver armbands, collars, and chains, while commoners wore clay, glass, and amber beads. Just a few decades ago, solid metal chains were all the rage in this country and many others. Now, however, the emphasis is on unique, eye-catching, free styles that suit the wearer. Today's jewelry trend is to express yourself, to find something unusual that suits you and to wear it with pizazz.

Perhaps the best thing about the current jewelry styles is that they are perfectly suited to the home crafter. The incredible range of bead-making supplies makes creating custom jewelry easier than ever. Color-tinted wire gives you a whole new palette of choices. Twisted wire is easy to make with specialty tools and is available premade from some wire suppliers. And many of the specialty wires, such as flat wire formerly available only to professional jewelry makers, is now easily accessible. Jigs—simple hole-drilled boards with pegs—are inexpensive tools used to create wonderful wire pattern links. Bead selections, also, have never been greater. Simple and intricate beads in an amazing variety of materials are available from around the world.

The pages that follow feature more than 70 pieces of bead and wire jewelry made by a diverse group of talented designers. Although each piece is accompanied by step-by-step instructions so you can exactly replicate a specific piece, you should also allow yourself the luxury of using this book as an inspirational guide for awakening the designer in yourself. If you don't feel ready to begin designing your own jewelry, consider making simple variations of your favorite project: small changes such as using a different gauge of a wire or another type of bead can create a completely different look. Soon you'll have the confidence to follow your muse. Special thanks to all of the contributing designers who shared their techniques, their inspirations, and hard-earned tips from years of experience.

Making bead and wire jewely is one of the simplest, most pleasant pastimes you will ever embark on. Even beginners can create a piece of respectable jewelry in an afternoon. If you've thumbed through the projects in this book and panic at the idea of making one, stop worrying. Making jewelry is just like learning a foreign language: At first all the words seem to run together in an indecipherable stream, but once you have a little vocabulary under your belt it's much easier to understand. Once you realize that a piece of jewelry is simply a combination of individual llnks (the same way a sentence is just a combination of individual words), you'll be well on your way to creating great jewelry.

BEAD & WIRE BASICS

Spool wire; handmade bead by Frantz Bead Company

MATERIALS

Fortunately, most materials used in making bead and wire jewelry are easy to find and fairly inexpensive. If you don't have a good jewelry supply store near you, the World Wide Web can be an excellent source for mail-order supply companies. A simple search using "bead and wire jewelry" as keywords will give you an ample list of potential sources; a more refined search using "bead sellers" or "wire jewelry making supplies" will give you even more choices.

Beads

Virtually everyone who has spent more than five minutes looking at an assortment of beads has fallen in love with them. Shape, material, translucency, surface decoration—there are almost more varieties than the mind can fathom. Some beads come with history; they echo a tradition of beadmaking that dates back for centuries. Other beads come with an

artist's soul in them, handcrafted as miniature works of art. Still other beads simply serve the moment's purpose—they're the right color, the right shape, the right price at the right time.

Many beads are sized and sold in millimeters, with the number indicating the size of the diameter in millimeters. Seed beads are the exception: they are sold in numbered sizes with the smallest beads receiving the highest numbers. As a precaution, always make sure your chosen wire will fit through your beads' holes. Some very large beads can have surprisingly small holes, and vice versa.

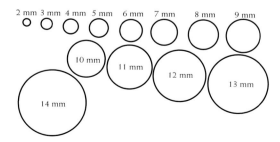

Figure 1. Standard bead sizes

Favorite Beads

Anyone who loves bead jewelry has their favorite beads, but could you describe why? Below, five professional bead makers share some of their favorite beads.

Frantz Beads

Bruce St. John Maher

Bill Glass

Michael Barley

Dee Snell

Wire

Since wire serves a twofold purpose for the jewelry in this book—both as a support system and as a decorative element—both of these considerations should be kept in mind when you shop for wire. Wire is available in any number of gauges and shapes as well as in different metals. Twenty-gauge wire is a common choice for many of the projects in this book, but 18 and 22 gauges are also good choices. Using other gauges is fine, just keep in mind that extremely thin wire may not be strong enough to support numerous heavy beads, while very thick wire may not cooperate when shaping small, intricate patterns.

Cost is another important consideration. Wire made from alloys (blends of less expensive metals) is an acceptable choice, especially for jewelry for everyday wear or for working a new design. Finding the perfect wire for a project is easy if you have a well-stocked jewelry supply shop nearby. If not, mailorder sources, many of whom are glad to send samples of their wares, are another good option.

Practice Wire is a great idea whenever you need experience working with a new pattern or when you plan to make a piece of jewelry from very expensive wire. Any inexpensive alloy wire will do, just be sure to choose something with a gauge and hardness similar to what you'll be using for the jewelry.

Twisted Wire is created when two lengths of wire are twisted together to create a beaded or rippled effect. Make your own twisted wire

with the pin vise tool shown on page 14. Some wire companies sell lengths of pretwisted wire.

Colored Metal Wire is available in a wide variety of colors from several manufacturers. Various colors can be mixed together in the same piece of jewelry or you can mix a color with your favorite metal. The number of special effects you can achieve is incredible, just be sure you choose beads that complement your wire instead of competing with it.

Colored Plastic Wire. Remember how much fun it was to make your own jewelry from colorful telephone wire when you were a teenager? Well, now it's even more fun. The colors are better and this wire has significantly more memory to it. The wire is actually made from a colored plastic coating around a metal center. Be sure to choose a design that echoes the fun, festive feel of plastic wire, and always check with your supplier to be sure the center wire isn't lead.

Square Wire. Although most of the projects in this book are made with common round wire, a few, such as the earrings on page 111, are made from square wire, which creates a completely different look. Some designers alternate links of round, flat, and twisted wire with stunning results.

Above: flat and twisted wire; center top: colored metal wire

Findings

Findings are the backbone for many types of jewelry. They include necklace and bracelet clasps, ear wires and posts, pin backings, as well as head pins and eye pins. Some findings, such as pin backings, won't show in the finished piece, so quality is the only consideration when shopping for them. Other findings, such as head pins and eye pins, will show in the finished piece so you should make every effort to find them in wire colors and gauges that work well with the rest of your materials.

Head pins and eye pins are frequently used findings. Head pins have flat bottoms that act as a stopper for a bead, while an eye pin has a loop on one end that acts as a stopper for a bead. Loops are then formed at the other end of the wire, close to the bead, and are used to attach this link to other links. In both cases, choose extra-long pins if you plan to add more than one bead. It's easy to trim off excess wire but there's nothing to be done when there's not enough..

Jump rings are another popular finding. These simple rings are great for connecting links. They can be found in a variety of different sizes and in many types of wire, or you can make your own by simply wrapping a length of wire around a nail or knitting needle and then cutting through the spirals. Always open and close jump rings by separating the ring sideways at its cut; pulling the ends straight out can undermine the strength of the wire and cause breakage.

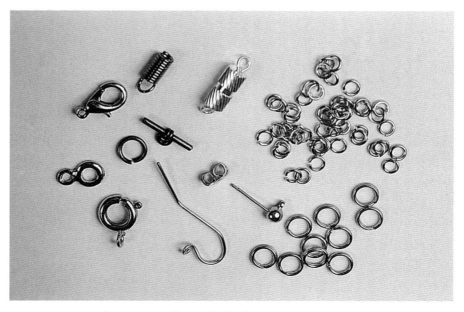

An assortment of commercially made findings

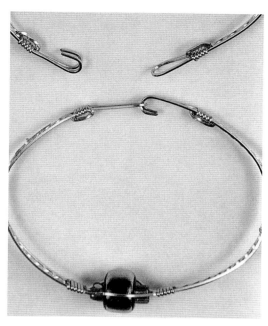

Sometimes separate clasp findings aren't necessary, as in the case of the wire-wrap bracelets (above) and the pendant (above right), which feature built-in findings.

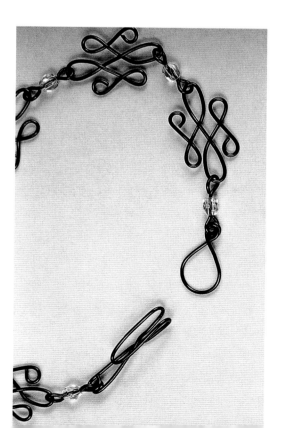

Findings can also be fashioned out of wire, either as simple hook-and-eye shapes (above) or in more elaborate patterns (left).

Tools

Wire Cutters. A good pair of wire cutters is essential to making the jewelry in this book. Since you will often need to cut wire in very small spaces, bigger is definitely not better. Pointed ends will give you even more control.

Files. Fine metal files are used to smooth out the rough edges of cut wire ends. Since unfiled ends can easily snag your favorite garments, fight all temptations to skip this step.

Pin Vises. This simple tool allows you to create lengths of twisted wire in just minutes. Simply insert each wire end into a vise,

tighten, and twist. Alternatively, two lengths of the same wire can be twisted together or you can twist two different colors of wire together.

Pliers. Pliers are a bead and wire jewelry maker's best friend. Round-nose, needle-nose, and flat-nose pliers are the three most used types, although other, more specialized types of pliers can be found. Look for a smooth edge (not a serrated one) on the inside of the pliers' jaws to prevent damage to your wire as you work. Inexpensive pliers are fine for beginners; if wire jewelry becomes your life passion you can easily trade up.

Jigs. Lots of wire jewelry can be made without ever using a jig, but it's a lifesaver when you're making a piece that uses multiple links made in the same shape. Pages 124-126 contain a nice variety of jig patterns, and your local jewelry shop probably has books that have even more. Jigs are also a good design tool: just play around with some inexpensive wire and different peg placements to create your own wire patterns.

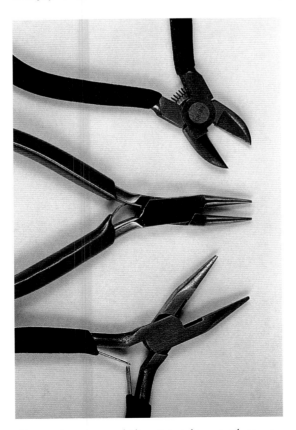

Above, wire cutters and pliers; top right, a simple pin vise

Work Spaces

A jewelry maker's work space can be as simple as a corner of the kitchen table or as elaborate as a dedicated studio room. While hefty investments are unnecessary, you may find the following suggestions helpful.

- **Contributing designer Geri Omohundro** keeps a desk pad of ¼-inch (3 mm) graph paper on her work table. "I've marked off 1-inch (2.5 cm) increments up to 8 inches (20 cm) so I can easily check my measurements and spacing as I work."

- **Contributing designer Susan Kinney** sorts her beads by color and places them in small ceramic bowls. "The bowls look like part of my home's decor and the presorted colors make the design process more fun."

- **Contributing designer Lilli Brennan** uses a plastic container with a domed lid to store samples of each jig pattern she's designed. When she's working on a new project, she inverts the domed lid and lines up jig links around the lid's ridge.

WHAT'S IN A NAME?

A popular dictionary defines a jig as "a device for guiding a tool or holding machine work in place." For many wire jewelry artists, though, that definition falls a little short. Several years ago, jewelry maker Marj Helwig became fascinated with wire links, but she was also frustrated with her inability to consistently make the same components by hand. Marj's son Gary made a wooden prototype in his basement to his mom's specs. The jig worked so well and so many of Marj's friends wanted one, that an entrepreneurial venture seemed a natural next step. What to name Marj's invention? Given her last name, "WigJig" seemed the natural choice.

Five years and six custom jigs later, WigJigs are a family business. Ideas for their specialty jigs originate from frustrations and inspirations in their own jewelry making. The necklace on page 74, for example, inspired the development of two specialty jigs. The Helwigs offer jig classes and are thrilled to receive letters and photos from jewelry designers around the country. "Making jig links really isn't hard to do," says Suzanne Helwig. "Good results generally require only two to four hours of practice."

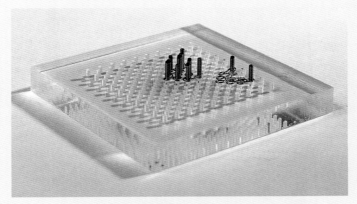

TECHNIQUES

Basic Links

In addition to the jig links described on page 14, there are several basic links that are commonly used in bead and wire jewelry making. If you're new to jewelry making, try to keep your frustration at bay as you develop your wire-bending skills. The basic techniques are simple, but practice and patience are required before you'll see professional results.

Jump Rings. These wire circles are frequently used to connect short links. The only trick to using jump rings is to open them from side to side, not straight apart, which will weaken the wire. (See figure 2.) It's tempting to use your fingernails to open the rings, but if you tire of splitting your fingernails, use two pairs of pliers instead.

Figure 2

Bead Loop Links. These links are often used in alternating patterns with other links. Begin by making a loop at one end of the wire around your round-nose pliers. Slide on a bead (or two), then make a second loop against the bead at the other end of the wire. Trim off any excess wire. Be sure to tighten any gaps in the loops after you've attached your links.

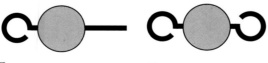

Figure 3   *Figure 4*

Twisted Wire Loop/Bead Links. These links are a simple variation of the loop/bead link. Begin by bending one end of a wire length at a 90-degree angle with chain-nose pliers (figure 5). Grasp the wires near the bend with round-nose pliers and wrap the wire around the top jaw of the pliers with your other hand (figure 6). Remove the pliers and reinsert them with the pliers' lower jaw inside the loop (figure 7). Use your other hand to wrap the wire around several times at a right angle at the base of the loop. Slide on one or more beads and repeat at the other end. Trim off any excess wire. Attach these links to other links with jump rings; alternatively, slide the loop of a connecting link onto the newly formed loop in figure 5 before continuing with the step shown in figure 6.

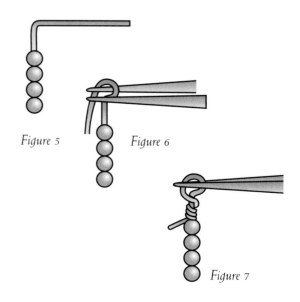

Figure 5   *Figure 6*

Figure 7

THE PROJECTS

CHOKER AND EARRING SET

Besides their beauty, clear glass beads provide the added bonus of showing the wire running through them, adding an extra dimension in visual interest. Designer tip: "Play with different arrangements of jig pegs to create original wire designs, then incorporate the links in necklaces, bracelets, earrings, and pins."

DESIGNER: LILLI BRENNAN

MATERIALS

- 22-inch (56 cm) length of 20-gauge wire
- 18 6 mm beads
- Clasp findings
- 16 eye pins
- Earring wires
- 2 head pins

TOOLS

- Wire cutters
- Round-nose pliers
- Jig

INSTRUCTIONS

1. Cut 17 1¼-inch (3.2 cm) lengths of wire and make a small loop with the round-nose pliers on one end of each of them. Arrange your jig in the pattern in figure 1 on page 124.

2. Make a loop on one end of a 1¼-inch wire length and attach it to the jig's first peg, then go around the second, third, and fourth pegs. Repeat with the remaining 16 1¼-inch lengths.

3. Slide a bead onto an eye pin. Make a loop on the other end of the wire close to the bead and trim off any excess wire. Repeat with the remaining 15 eye pins.

4. Set two of the jig links formed in step 2 aside, then connect the remaining jig links to the bead links in an alternating pattern. Close any gaps in the loops with pliers and add clasp findings.

5. To make the earrings, attach a jig link to each ear wire, turning them in opposite directions. Drop a bead onto each head pin and form a loop close to the bead. Trim off any excess wire and attach the bead link to the jig link.

WIRE WRAP CHOKER

This choker is made from the same basic design as the bracelets on pages 34 and 87. Although the technique is not difficult, the choker can be challenging because of the length of wire it requires. Designer tip: "Develop the patience of a saint and the dexterity of a six-fingered monkey before tackling this project!"

DESIGNER & BEAD ARTIST: GERI OMOHUNDRO

MATERIALS

- 36-inch (92 cm) length of 21-gauge, full-hard, square silver wire
- 15½-inch (39 cm) length of 18-gauge, dead-soft, square silver wire
- 30-inch (76 cm) length of 21-gauge, half-round, silver wire
- Dichroic glass bead
- 2 silver Thai tube beads
- 6 4 mm Czech round beads

*Note: These lengths will make a 16-inch choker; allow for extra wire if a longer choker is desired.

TOOLS

- Wire cutter
- Pin vise or c-clamp
- Flat-nose pliers
- Round-nose pliers
- Tape
- Emery board
- Polishing cloth

INSTRUCTIONS

1. Place one end of the 36-inch hard wire in the pin vise or c-clamp and straighten by pulling the polishing cloth down the length of the wire several times.

2. Place the 15½-inch soft wire in the vise or c-clamp ¼ inch (6 mm) and grasp with the flat-nose pliers from the other end. Twist until you have a nice, even, fine patten, leaving the ends untwisted.

3. Bend the 36-inch wire in half using the round-nose pliers, forming a loop about half way up the pliers to form one end of the choker.

4. Add the twisted wire to the middle, holding in ¼ inch from the loop end. Wrap tape around the wire bundle about 2 inches (5 cm) from the loop and once on the other end to keep the wires from twisting as you wrap them.

5. Cut the half-round wire into manageable lengths (about 6 inches, 15 cm). Make an angled bend at the end of each length with the end of the flat-nose pliers. Hook one bend over the bundle ½ inch (6 mm) from the loop (¼ inch from the twisted wire end). Grasp the hook and wire bundle with flat-nose pliers and, as you keep the bundle straight, firmly wrap half-round wire around the bundle five times, ending in the back. Snip the half-round wire and bevel-file the end with the emery board. Press the wire against the bundle.

6. Grasp the end of the twisted wire and bend back over the inside of your first wrap. While bending, bend the tip of the wire down, then press against the wrap to secure the end of the twisted wire.

7. Add two more wire wraps about an inch (2.5 cm) away from the previous wrap. At this point you should be about 3 inches (7.5 cm) into the project. Remove the tape on the 5-inch (12.5 cm) mark.

8. Use the round-nose pliers to bend one of the outer wires down at a 90-degree angle from the bundle about ½ inch beyond the last wire wrap. Make a second bend so that the wire parallels the bundle. Slip a 4 mm Czech bead onto the wire, then make a bend back up to the wire bundle.

9. Tape the wire bundle in two places again to hold the wires straight. Wire wrap ½ inch beyond the bead using half-round wire. Repeat steps 8 and 9 twice more. Note: It is tedious to tape and untape, but it's necessary to keep the bundle straight.

10. Add another wire wrap ½ inch beyond the last one. (There should be three beads on the choker now.) Bend the outer wires slightly away from the bundle and add the tube beads and the dichroic bead. Using round-nose pliers, shape the outer wires so that they follow the contour of the beads. Tape the wire bundle in several places and wire wrap snugly against the beads you just added.

11. To make the second side of the choker, wire wrap at the same intervals, adding the Czech beads as you go. After the end wrap, bend the twisted wire back over the bundle as directed in step 6. About ½ inch of wire should remain at the end. Pinch these wires together with the flat-nose pliers and snip to even. File the square edge, then grasp with round-nose pliers and make a bend to form a J that will serve as the clasp for the loop at the other end.

12. Shape the choker by grasping the ends and slowly bending them toward each other as you brace the middle against a table. Use your fingers to keep tension on the whole piece to prevent kinking and to form a nice, rounded oval. File the wire ends either bevel or square to prevent sharp spots.

Faceted Beads Necklace

What looks like an intricate, expensive necklace to the casual observer is actually a fairly simple, inexpensive piece to create. The use of faceted, glass beads increases the allure.

MATERIALS

- 10 8 mm beads
- 60½-inch (1.54 m) length of 20-gauge gold wire
- Clasp findings

TOOLS

- Wire cutters
- Round-nose pliers
- Jig with regular-size pegs and extra-large peg or nylon spacer

INSTRUCTIONS

1. Cut nine 4½-inch (11.5 cm) lengths of wire. Make a loop with the round-nose pliers at one end of each wire.

2. Set up the jig as shown in figure 2 on page 124. Attach the loop around the first peg and wrap the wire around one side of the large peg and then around the other peg and back around the large peg. Finish by wrapping around the first peg. Repeat eight times with the remaining wire lengths.

3. Cut 10 2-inch (5 cm) lengths of wire. Make a loop about ¼ inch (3 mm) from the ends and make two to three wire wraps at the base of the loop. Slide on a bead so that it rests against the wire wraps.

4. Attach each of the jig links to one of the half-formed bead links by slipping the loop in the bead link onto the jig link through the gap in the loop that went over the start peg.

5. Form a loop on the other ends of the bead links about ⅛ inch (3 mm) away from the bead. Slide a jig link into the loop, then secure with two to three wire wraps between the bead and the loop. Add clasp findings to each end.

DESIGNER: LILLI BRENNAN

Rococo Necklace

Copper wire links that have been flattened with a jewelry hammer combine with lampwork beads to create a piece with rococo flair. These directions make a 20-inch (50 cm) necklace, but you can easily change the length by adding or deleting figure-eight units from the ends of the necklace.

MATERIALS

- 16 mm center lamp-work bead
- 2 6 mm lampwork beads
- 4 6 mm beads
- 20-gauge copper or brass wire
- Clasp findings

TOOLS

- Wire cutters
- Round-nose pliers
- Jig
- Soft mallet or jewelry hammer

INSTRUCTIONS

1. Cut seven 2-inch (5 cm) lengths of wire. Slide a bead onto each wire length. Fold a loop in the wire close to the bead at each end and make several wraps. Trim off any excess wire.

2. Cut four 6-inch (15 cm) lengths of wire and make a small loop with the round-nose pliers on one end of each of them. Set up your jig, using the pattern in figure 3, page 124, as a guide. Make a loop at one end of the wire around round-nose pliers. Place the loop on the left peg and then wrap as shown in the jig pattern.

3. Flatten the jig links by covering them with a soft cloth and then pounding them gently with a soft mallet or jewelry hammer.

4. Cut 20 1-inch (2.5 cm) lengths of wire and use the pliers to form figure-eight shapes with them by bending one end in a loop toward the middle from the right and the other end in a loop toward the middle from the left. Leave a small gap in the end of the loops.

5 Use the figure-eight links to connect the bead and jig links. Create two chains containing five figure-eight shapes and attach one chain to each end of the necklace. Close the gaps in the figure eights and add clasp findings.

MATERIALS

- Long cylindrical bead drilled from top to bottom (lengthwise)
- 2 smaller matching beads for earrings
- 40-inch length of 21-gauge gold-filled square dead-soft wire
- 7-inch (18 cm) length of 22-gauge gold-filled square dead-soft wire
- 2-foot (1.8 m) length of 18-gauge or 20-gauge gold-filled half-round wire
- 12-inch (31 cm) length of 26-gauge gold-filled round wire (doublecheck to make sure this wire is thin enough to fit through your beads)
- Gold-filled French hooks
- Masking tape

TOOLS

- Small flush wire cutter
- Round, chain-, and flat-nose pliers
- Steel ruler
- Pin vise or wire twister
- Laundry marking pen
- Small mini-mandrel or knitting needle

INSTRUCTIONS FOR PENDANT

1. Cut the 21-gauge wire into four 10-inch (25 cm) lengths.

2. To make the pendant, twist two 10-inch lengths of wire together with the pin vise. Place the twisted wires and the two remaining single 10-inch wires together in a bundle with the two twisted wires on the outside. Mark the center of the bundle with a laundry pen. Secure with masking tape. (Note: If you've invested in a hemostat, place masking tape on the clamps so the gold won't be scratched.)

3. Remove the tape and place the center of the bundle of wires on your index finger. Place your other index finger on top of the marked spot and twirl the wires into a 360-degree turn with a single movement of the hand and wrist. Be careful to hold the bundle of wires together at all times. (During this process the wires should not be taped or held with a hemostat.) After completing the turn, your bundle should look like a very loose W.

4. While holding the bundle together, gently shape up the pendant by bending the four wires on the right side up and then bending the four wires on the left side up until the wires cross each other on top. Continue shaping the wire to create a frame that is the size of your bead.

5. Take the 26-gauge wire and make a hook about 1-inch from the end of the wire with round-nose pliers. Run the hook of the wire through the circle at the bottom of the pendant. Make several wraps with this wire and secure it around the base of the 26-gauge wire. (Tip: If the circle tends to close up, use a steel dental pick to open it up.) Now string your bead onto the 26-gauge wire and fit the bead into the pendant frame.

6. Mark the upper end of the frame with the laundry pen to allow for space for the bead. Carefully uncross and straighten the upper wires on the right side of then pendant, then straighten the upper wires on the left side of the pendant.

7. Make a hook with the tip of your flat-nose pliers about 1 inch from the end of your 18-gauge half-round wire. Put the hook over the laundry pen mark above the bead and began wrapping the 18-gauge half round

SCULPTED WIRE BEAD SETTINGS

Custom wire settings are a wonderful way to showcase your favorite beads. The techniques are simple, but you may want to rehearse them with an inexpensive practice wire before trying them with the more expensive gold-filled wires shown here.

DESIGNER: PRESTON J. REUTHER

wire toward the top of the pendant. Make four complete wraps around the top of the pendant to hold the wires together.

8. Measure approximately 1 inch from the top of the lowest wrap of the bundle and bend the wire back 90 degrees with flat-nose pliers. Measure the distance from the top of the wraps to the bend and measure the same distance on the other side of the bend. Cut the end wires at the measured point. Now bend the bail wires back with flat-nose pliers until they touch the back of the pendant.

9. Align the ends of the cut wires right above the top wrap wire. You may have to cut more wire off if your wires are too long. They must be straight and must be right above the line of your upper wrap wire. Begin wrapping again, securing the bail wires together with the pendant. Continue with four or five more complete wraps and cut the wire off in the back of the pendant. Designer tips: When judging the length of the bail, remember that a longer pendant will require a longer bail. Try to err on the size of too large because a bail that is too small will not fit on your chain. Also, remember to cut your wrap wires in the back of your pendant so that the cut ends won't show.

10. Run a round, steel mini-mandrel through the bail to open the bail up a little, if needed.

Instructions for Earrings

1. Follow the instructions above with the following changes for the pendant. Using the 22-gauge wire, start making your wraps with the half-round wire at the top of the frame. Make three wraps. Stop and carefully cut the outer twisted wire on each side of the earring, cutting right above the last wrap.

2. Wrap one full wrap with half round. Stop and cut the outer untwisted wire on each side of the earring, cutting right above the last wrap. Wrap one more full wrap with half-round wire. Stop and cut the inner untwisted wire on each side of the earring, cutting right above the last wrap. Now make one full wrap again with the half round. You should have a nice tapering affect, called stepping. After making your last wrap, cut your wrap wire in the back of the earring.

3. Clip the 26-gauge wire even with the top of the wrap. You should only have the two twisted inner wires coming up from the wraps. Clip the two remaining twisted wires about ⅜ inch (9 mm) from the top of the upper wrap. Make a small round loop with the round-nose pliers, bending the loop backward. Before fully closing the loop, turn the small O ring on the French hook a with your flat-nose pliers so the flat side of the O is facing the front of the earring. Insert the O of your French hooks and carefully close the loop by pressing the end wires of the loop onto the back of the earring.

TEAL COILS HAIR CLIP

The intriguing wire effect in this hair clip is created by wrapping a length of colored wire around a think dowel to create coils and then repeating the process to create coils of coils.

MATERIALS

- Metal triangular hair clip
- 22-gauge colored wire in desired color
- Fiber optic glass bead with large hole

TOOLS

- Needle- or flat-nose pliers
- Thin dowel rod or nail
- Glue (optional)

DESIGNER: SHARON HESSOLIN

INSTRUCTIONS

1. Open the hair clip. Wrap the top of the hair clip with wire. Glue underside if needed to hold it on the ends. Tightly wrap the wire around a the dowel until you have a coil about 12 inches (30 cm) long, leaving a 1- to 2-inch (2.5 to 5 cm) tail on each end of the coil.

2. Slide the large-holed bead onto the coil and position it near the center. Wrap the coiled wire around the dowel to create coiled coils and repeat the process until you have the desired effect.

3. Attach the coil to one end of the hair clip by slipping a short length of matching wire through one of the coils near the end and then wrapping the wire around the hair clip to anchor in place. Repeat on the other end. With larger clips you may need to anchor the coils in the center of the clip, also.

RUNE BEAD NECKLACES

Designer Geri Omohundro calls these pendant beads rune beads because their shape and feel remind her of their historical namesakes. A routered groove along the edge provides a place the lay the wire for a clean design.

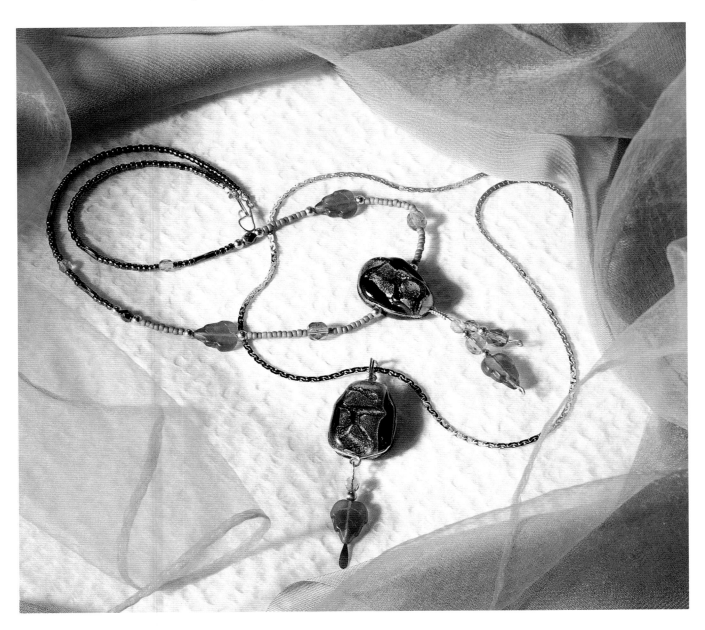

DESIGNER & BEAD ARTIST: GERI OMOHUNDRO

MATERIALS

FOR NECKLACE AT FRONT

- Flat, square-edge bead
- 21-gauge square wire the length of the distance around the bead plus 2 inches (5 cm)
- 3-inch (7.5 cm) length of half-round 21-gauge wire
- Gold-tone teardrop paddle for drop
- 3 mm gold-filled round bead
- Leaf bead
- 4 mm Czech bead

TOOLS

- Flat-nose pliers
- Round-nose pliers
- Wire cutters
- Emery board
- Tape

INSTRUCTIONS

1. Rout the bead edge as described in the instructions on page 33.

2. Grasp the center of the square wire with round-nose pliers and make a small loop. This loop will go against the bottom center of the drop bead.

3. Fit the wire against the bottom of the bead and the center loop. Press the wire into the groove, fitting it tightly along the curves.

4. Bend each wire at a right angle at the center top of the bead with flat-nose pliers. Tape the wires to stabilize them.

5. Begin the wrap with half-round wire by making a hook in the end with flat-nose pliers, then catch it against the bundled square wire. Wrap around twice. Remove the tape.

6. Form a hanging loop with square pliers by bending the wire toward the back of the pendant. Make a second bend so that the wires point down. Note: The pendant will hang better if you make the first bend at a 120-degree angle and the second bend at a 60-degree angle.

7. Place the square wire against the half-round wire wrap and wrap with the square wire, catching the bent down wires in the next several wraps. Trim the wire, leaving a $\frac{1}{8}$-inch (3 mm) tail. File the wire end and tuck it against the bundle.

8. Slide the leaf bead, the gold bead, and the Czech bead onto the teardrop paddle. Bend the top $\frac{1}{4}$ inch (6 mm) at a right angle with flat-nose pliers. Start a loop near the end of the round-nose pliers and close the loop with round-nose pliers.

9. String your favorite chain through the loop at the top of the bead and enjoy.

MATERIALS

FOR NECKLACE AT BACK

- Flat, square-edged, routered bead
- 3-inch (7.5 cm) length of gold-filled 21-gauge wire
- 3 3 mm gold-filled round beads
- 2 4 mm Czech beads
- 2 6 mm Czech beads
- Leaf bead
- Seed and accent beads for necklace
- Nylon beading cord
- Necklace clasp findings
- 4 crimp beads

TOOLS

- Flat-nose pliers
- Round-nose pliers
- Wire cutters
- Emery board

INSTRUCTIONS

1. Rout the bead edge as described in the instructions on page 33.

2. Press the wire around the bead, fitting it into the routed groove. (The wires can be offset at the bottom of the bead.) Bend each wire at a right angle at the bottom center of the bead with flat-nose pliers. Tape the wires to stabilize.

3. Begin wrapping by making a hook in the end of the half-round wire with the flat-nose pliers and then bending the wires slightly away from each other. Slip the beads onto the longer wire in this order: one 4 mm Czech bead, one gold bead, one 6 mm Czech bead, one gold bead, and one leaf bead. Make a finishing loop by bending the end of the wire ¼ inch (6 mm) at a right angle with flat-nose pliers. Round over on the end of the pliers.

4. Add beads to the shorter wire in this order: one 4 mm Czech bead, one gold bead, and one 6 mm Czech bead. Make finishing loop as described at the end of step 3. Set the pendant aside.

5. To make the necklace, cut a piece of nylon beading cord to 4 inches (10 cm) longer than you want your finished necklace to be. Tape one end of the beading cord onto a flat work surface.

6. String seed beads onto the cord until you come to the area that will rest against your collar bone, then begin mixing in accent beads. Add the bead pendant when you reach the middle of the cord and then repeat your beading pattern on the other side. Check to make sure the patterns are duplicated and that the sides are even.

7. Add two crimp beads on one end of the beading cord. Slide on one side of the necklace fastener. Thread the nylon back through both crimp beads, come back over one bead, and then through the other crimp bead one more time to lock in the cord. Gently crimp the beads with flat-nose (or crimping) pliers.

8. Untape the other end of the necklace and slide the beads toward the finished end. Slide on two crimp beads, the other half of the fastener, and thread the cord as you did in step 7. Crimp the beads and trim off any excess cord very close to the crimp beads.

ROUTERING BEADS

Routering a groove around your favorite bead is an easy way to create stunning, one of-a-kind pendants. Start with a flat, square-edged bead at least $\frac{3}{16}$-inch (5 mm) thick. (A lesser thickness is prone to chipping.) Working with a jewelry grinding bit and a compatible handheld power tool, set the bit so the groove will cut in the middle of the bead's edge. Grind into the edge of the bead just the thickness of your chosen wire. Clean off any dust, then use the bead to inspire a great piece of jewelry!

The grooves hold the wire secure while allowing you to make almost invisible wire wraps. If you're a glass beadmaker, you can make your own bead by using your paddle to marver the bead flat as you work it in the flame. (Hint: Working with a black base keeps the black soft longer.) Marver the bead flat until you reach the desired size, then add a strip of dichroic color. As the color sinks into the back, continue to marver both sides, keeping the bead flat with square sides. Don't worry about perfect symmetry: each bead should be unique.

— **Geri Omohundro**

WIRE WRAP BRACELETS

These simple bracelets are a great way to show off your favorite specialty beads. Make them in gold or silver, and vary the bead choices to create unique pieces. A tip from the designer: "Check each wrap to make sure you're starting them all from the same side. It's pretty easy to flip the bracelet over at the halfway point and wrap from the wrong side."

DESIGNER & BEAD ARTIST GERI OMOHUNDRO

MATERIALS

- 15-inch (38 cm) length of 21-gauge gold-filled, half-hard square wire or 21-gauge full hard square silver wire

- 6½-inch (16.5 cm) length of 20-gauge gold-filled, dead-soft square wire or 18-gauge dead-soft square silver wire

- 10-inch (25 cm) length of 21-gauge gold-filled, half-round wire or 21-gauge half-round silver wire

- Large focal bead (a dichroic glass bead was used here)

- 4 accent beads

- Tape

*These wire lengths will make a 7-inch (18 cm) bracelet; allow extra wire for larger sizes.

TOOLS

- Wire cutters
- Vise or c-clamp
- Flat-nose pliers
- Round-nose pliers
- Emery board
- Polishing cloth

INSTRUCTIONS

1. Place one end of the 15-inch length of wire in the vise and straighten by pulling the polishing cloth down the length of the wire several times.

2. Place the 6½-inch length of wire in the vise ¼ inch (3 mm) and grasp it with the flat-nose pliers ¼ inch from the other end. Twist until you have a nice, even, fine pattern and leave the ends untwisted.

3. Bend the 15-inch length of wire in half using the round-nose pliers, making a loop about half of the way up the pliers. Add the twisted wire to the middle of the wire, holding ¼ inch in from the loop end. Wrap tape around the wire bundle about 2 inches (5 cm) and 5 inches (13 cm) from the loop to prevent the wires from twisting as you wrap them.

4. Using the 10-inch wire, make an angled bend at the end of the flat-nose pliers. Hook the bend over the bundle ½ inch (6 mm) from the loop (¼ inch from the twisted wire end). Grasp the hook and wire bundle with the flat-nose pliers and firmly wrap the half-round wire around the bundle five times, keeping the bundle straight and ending in the back. Snip the half-round wire and bevel-file the end with the emery board, then press the wire against the bundle.

5. Grasp the end of the twisted wire and bend back over the inside of your first wrap. As you work, bend the tip of the wire down, then press against the wrap to secure the end of the twisted wire.

6. Add two more wire wraps about 1 inch apart. You should have one wrap about ½ inch from the ends, one wrap close to each side of the bead area, and one wrap centered between the end and the bead wrap.

7. At this point you are about 3 inches (7.5 cm) into the project. Remove the tape on the 5-inch mark. Slightly bend out the outer wires and slide your beads along the center twisted wire. Check and center the beads, then pull the wire bundle snug around them. You may wish to use round- or flat-nose pliers to help you make a symmetrical bend around the beads, depending on their shape.

(Continued on page 37)

EVERGREEN WIRE & CRYSTAL BEADS NECKLACE

Small crystal beads and jig links made from a dark green wire create an elegant combination that can easily be adapted to earrings, a bracelet, or a longer necklace.

DESIGNER: LILLI BRENNAN

MATERIALS

- 12 4 mm crystal beads
- 37-inch (94 cm) length of 20-gauge colored wire

TOOLS

- Wire cutters
- Round-nose pliers
- Jig
- Emery board

INSTRUCTIONS

1. Cut 11 2-inch (5 cm) lengths of wire. Make a loop with the round-nose pliers at one end of each wire.

2. Set up the jig as shown in figure 4 on page 124. Attach the loop around the first peg and wrap the wire around the pegs. Repeat ten times with the remaining wire lengths.

3. Cut 12 ¾-inch (2 cm) lengths of wire. Make a loop about ¼ inch (3 mm) from the end of a wire length. Slide on a bead and make a second loop that rests against the bead. Trim any excess wire and repeat 11 times with the remaining wire lengths.

4. Attach each of the jig links to the bead links, then remove any gaps in the bead loops.

5. Cut two 3-inch (7.5 cm) lengths of wire and make clasp findings from the jig patterns in figure 5 on page 124. Trim off any excess wire and file ends.

(Continued from page 35)

8. Tape the wire bundle in two places again to hold the wires straight. Wire wrap next to the beads to hold them tight. Center the next wire wrap between the bead wrap and the end wrap. The end wrap should be ¼ inch in from the end of the twisted wire.

9. Bend the twisted wire back over the bundle as in step 5. About ½ inch of wire should remain at the end. Pinch these together with the flat-nose pliers and snip to even. File the edge square, then grasp with round-nose pliers and bend the wire into a J shape to form the clasp.

10. Shape the bracelet to form an oval by grasping the ends and slowly bending them toward each other as you brace the middle against a table, using your fingers to keep tension on the whole piece so that it doesn't kink as you work.

CAGED BEADS BRACELET

Wire cages are a beautiful way to show off your spectacular beads. For added variety, try experimenting by caging some of the beads with twisted wire or cages in different shapes. A matching necklaces is simple to make: just keep adding caged and accent beads until you achieve the desired length. For matching earrings, attach a caged bead to an earring finding.

DESIGNER: MAMI LAHER

MATERIALS

- 12 feet (10.8 m) of 18- or 20-gauge round wire for cages
- 5 or more 10 x 13 mm oval beads or 10 mm round beads with openings large enough for 18-gauge wire to fit through
- 3 feet (2.7 m) of 18-gauge round wire for center pins and jump rings
- 6 8 mm metal beads
- Clasp

TOOLS

- Round-nose pliers
- Chain-nose pliers
- Flush cutters

INSTRUCTIONS

1. For each caged bead, cut a 9-inch (2.3 cm) length of 18- or 20-gauge round wire. Make loops at both ends of the wire, holding the wire one-third of the way into the mouth of round-nose pliers.

2. Using flat-nose pliers, coil the wire halfway from each end to form a symmetrical, S-shaped scroll. Hold the middle of the scroll with the pliers and bend the top half of the scroll onto the bottom half so that the two halves are stacked.

3. Grab the center of one of the coils with the flat-nose pliers and pull gently, stretching the coil out about ⅜ inch (1 cm). Repeat with the other coil in the opposite direction.

4. Pry the cage open slightly where the gap between the wires is widest and insert an oval bead. Close the gap by bending the wires back into place.

5. Repeat steps 1-4 to make the remaining cages. Note: This bracelet measures 8 inches (20 cm) and uses 5 caged beads. For extra length, simply add an additional caged bead.

6. Cut a 1¾-inch (4.5 cm) length of 18-gauge wire for each cage and insert through the center of the caged bead. Make loops at each end of the cage from the protruding wire by bending the wire at a 45-degree angle (or slightly more) and then grabbing the wire end with pliers and bending to complete the loop.

7. Thread each metal bead onto a 1¼-inch (3.2 cm) length of 18-gauge wire. Make loops at one end of the bead from the protruding wire as you did in the end of step 6.

8. Connect the caged bead units to the metal accent beads and close the loops with pliers. Attach clasp findings to finish.

SILK SWIRL NECKLACE

Here's a festive necklace for steppin' out on the town. The silk ribbon knots will work with just about any style of necklace—just be sure to choose a width that complements your wire gauge.

MATERIALS

- 4 foot (3.6 m) length of copper 16-gauge wire
- 4 foot length of black 16-gauge wire
- 8 14 mm black beads (be sure the hole will accommodate the wire)
- 4-foot (3.6 m) length of narrow silk ribbon in coordinating color

TOOLS

- Wire cutters
- Round-nose pliers
- Jewel glue
- Jig
- Nylon pliers

INSTRUCTIONS

1. Cut four 12-inch (31 cm) lengths from each of the wires. Set up the jig using the pattern in figure 6 on page 124. Work each wire length around the pegs in a counterclockwise direction, leaving a ¼-inch (3 mm) open loop at the end and clipping off any excess wire.

2. Add a small amount of glue to the inside of a bead and insert it onto the wire end in the center of the scroll. Repeat with the remaining beads.

3. Alternating colors, connect the scrolls together by gently placing the end loop of one scroll over the middle portion of the outside curve of the next scroll. With nylon pliers, gently close the loops except the one on the far left.

4. Cut the ribbon into 6-inch lengths. Attach each ribbon to one of the connecting loops with a square knot. Clip the ribbons to a pleasing length (1-½-inch lengths were used here).

5. Fasten the necklace by placing the open-ended outer loop over the beginning swirl at the nape of the neck.

DESIGN: SALLY WALTER

Simple Twist Dichroic Bead Earrings

These earrings make nice, quick projects if you like dangle earrings and want to use up some extra beads to complement other jewelry you've made. The dichroic glass beads look exceptionally lovely when combined with twisted wire.

Designer & Bead Artist: Geri Omohundro

MATERIALS

- 14-inch (36 cm) length of dead-soft 22-gauge wire
- 2 dichroic glass beads
- 6 3 mm gold-filled, round beads
- 2 ear wires

TOOLS

- Wire cutters
- Flat-nose pliers
- Round-nose pliers
- Pin vise or clamp

INSTRUCTIONS

1. Cut two pieces of wire 3½ inches (9 cm) long. Holding the wires together, place one end ¼ inch (3 mm) into the vise and twist, leaving ¼ inch untwisted at the other end. File the ends smooth and square.

2. Make a loop at one end by bending the wire at a right angle with the flat-nose pliers and then rolling the wire into a small loop with round-nose pliers.

3. Slide one gold bead, one dichroic bead, and another gold bead onto the wire so that they rest just above the loop.

4. Bend the wire with the end of the round-nose pliers 1¾ inch (4.5 cm) from the end into a relaxed, bobby-pin shape so that the ends are offset.

5. Slip on the ear wire, then slip on another gold bead. Make a finishing loop on the end and let the bead rest on top of the loop.

6. Repeat steps 1-5 for the second earring, mounting the second ear wire so that it mirror images the direction of the first ear wire.

Fancy Twist Dichroic Bead Earrings

These earrings are a simple variation of the earrings on page 42. Make a few extra sets and save them for gift-giving occasions.

MATERIALS

- 14-inch (36 cm) length of dead-soft 22-gauge wire
- 2 dichroic glass beads
- 6 3 mm gold-filled, round beads
- 4 Czech 4 mm round beads
- 2 ear wires
- 4 twisted oval or leaf beads

TOOLS

- Wire cutters
- Flat-nose pliers
- Round-nose pliers
- Pin vise or clamp

DESIGNER & BEAD ARTIST: GERI OMOHUNDRO

INSTRUCTIONS

1. Cut two pieces of wire 3½ inches (9 cm) long. Holding the wires together, place one end ¼ inch (3 mm) into the vise and twist, leaving ¼ inch untwisted at the other end. File the ends smooth and square.

2. Make a loop at one end by bending the wire at a right angle with the flat-nose pliers and then rolling the wire into a small loop with round-nose pliers.

3. Slide one Czech bead, one gold bead, one dichroic glass bead, another gold bead, and one twisted oval or leaf bead (in that order) down the wire until they rest just above the loop.

4. Bend the wire with the end of the round-nose pliers 1¾ inch (4.5 cm) from the end into a relaxed, bobby-pin shape so that the ends are offset. Slip on the ear wire.

5. Slide on one twisted oval or leaf bead, one gold bead, and one Czech bead (in that order). Make loop as before.

6. Repeat steps 1-5 for the second earring, mounting the second ear wire so that it mirror images the direction of the first ear wire.

CAPTURED BEADS NECKLACE

Warning: Do not make this necklace unless you're comfortable with people staring at your neck in public places! The center focal area featuring beads seemingly "captured" in a coil of colorful wire is easy to create, but will have onlookers staring at your neck and asking questions.

INSTRUCTIONS

1. Cut six 1½-inch (3.8 cm) lengths from the silver wire. Form a loop around the round-ose pliers at one end of a length of wire. Slide on a heart-shaped bead and make a small loop close to the bead at the other end. Trim off any excess wire. Repeat with the remaining lengths of wire.

2. Cut four 1¾-inch (4.5 cm) lengths from the silver wire. Form a loop around the round-nose pliers at one end of a length of wire. Slide on a bead and make a small loop close to the bead at the other end. Trim off any excess wire. Reeat with the remaining lengths of wire.

3. Cut two 1¼-inch (3.2 cm) lengths from the silver wire and two from the green wire and form S-shaped links by curving one end of the wire in toward the center point around the round-nose pliers and then curving the other end in toward the center point in the opposite direction. Repeat with the remaining lengths of wire.

4. Cut six 4½-inch (11.5 cm) lengths from the green wire. Set the jig in the pattern shown in figure 7 on page 124 and make six links. Trim any excess wire.

5. Cut six 6-inch (15 cm) lengths from the burgundy wire. Set the jig in the pattern shown in figure 8 on page 124 and make six links.

6. Cut a 30-inch (76 cm) length of green wire and coil it around the knitting needle. Remove the coil and spread it out slightly. Cut a 5½-inch (14 cm) length of silver wire and make a loop at one end with the round-nose pliers. String on one 8 mm bead, one square bead, 8 4 mm beads, another square bead, 8 more 4 mm beads, and one more square bead.

7. Slide the coil over the 4 mm beads so that it sits next to the 8 mm bead. Cut off any length of coil that protrudes beyond the last square bead. Add the remaining 8 mm bead and make a loop. Trim excess silver wire.

8. Assemble the links in this order: one silver S-link from step 3, one link from step 4, one heart-bead link, one link from step 5, one tube-bead link, one link from step 4, another tube-bead link, a link from step 5, a heart-bead link, a link from step 4, another heart-bead link, and a link from step 5. Make a second chain following the same pattern. Connect the step 5 links of each chain to the coiled link with green S-links. Add a clasp finding to each end.

CELESTIAL NECKLACE

The celestial charm and the wonderful blue dichroic glass beads were the inspiration for this project. The focal bead features a lightning bolt accent made from hammered wire. Designer Tip: When making a two-strand necklace, always use spacer bars which will help keep the strands straight, and remember to weight the inner strand with some large beads so it will hang evenly.

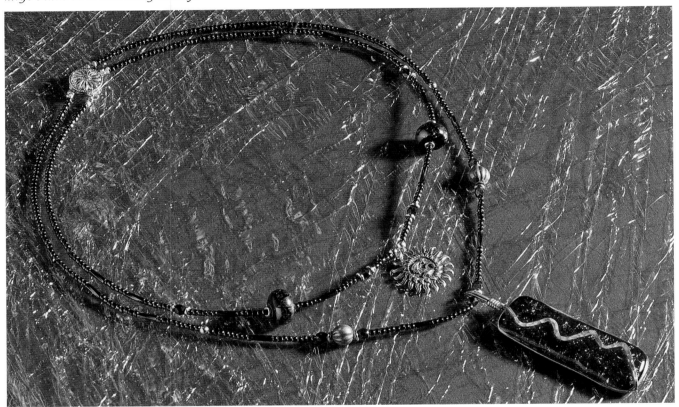

DESIGNER & BEAD ARTIST: GERI OMOHUNDO

INSTRUCTIONS

1. Rout a bead or glass pendant according to the instructions on page 33. Cut square wire to fit around bead plus 2 inches (5 cm). Press wire into groove, fitting it tightly along curves. Bend each wire at a right angle at top center of bead with flat-nose pliers. Tape wires to stabilize.

2. Begin wrap with half-round wire by making a hook in the end with flat-nose pliers, then catching it against the bundled square wire. Wrap around twice. Remove tape.

3. With square pliers, form a hanging loop by bending wire toward back of pendant. Make second bend so that wires are now headed down. You are basically making a square-cornered loop.

- Focal bead at least ¼ inch (3 mm) thick or fused glass pendant
- Several inches of 18-gauge dead-soft silver wire
- 21-gauge square silver wire
- 21-gauge half-round silver wire
- 2 spacer bars for beaded necklace
- Celestial sunflower sterling silver charm
- 2 round Thai silver beads
- Several 4 mm Czech beads
- Several 3 mm silver round beads
- Sterling silver 2-strand necklace clasp
- Silver tone crimp beads
- Seed beads & beading cord

TOOLS

- Wire cutters
- Flat- and round-nose pliers
- Small hammer
- Jeweler's anvil
- Emery board
- Soldering iron
- Lead-free solder
- Flux, wax, & tape

4. Determine where to trim the wire by placing it against the half-round wire wrap and allowing an extra ⅛ inch (1.5 mm). Wire wrap, catching the bent down wires in the next several wraps and leaving ⅛ inch bent ends out so the loop doesn't pull apart. Cut the half-round wire, file, and tuck against bundle.

5. Take the 18-gauge dead-soft wire and bend it into a zigzag shape using the round-nose pliers. Using a small hammer, pound it out gently on the jeweler's anvil. A special jeweler's hammer can help you achieve a rough or smooth surface.

6. Fit the wire onto the pendant, bending the end down over the edge and cutting where it meets the wire in the groove. Solder the first side in place by sparingly brushing it with flux and touching a slight drop of solder to make a welded joint. You want it to be secure but not obvious! Bend the other end down and repeat the process for a tight fit. Clean and polish the soldered joints with some wax so they won't oxidize.

7. Now you are ready to bead your pendant up into a two-strand necklace. Arrange your accent beads on a flat surface to create a satisfying design. Determine how long you'd like your finished strand to be and add 4 to 6 inches (10 to 15 cm) to that measurement to ease. Tape the ends of the beading cord to your work surface.

8. Add the seed beads to the cord. As you come to the place where the necklace will lay on your collarbone, add a spacer bar so the necklace will hang properly. Continue beading, adding the accent beads you have laid out. After you add the pendant, make sure you mirror image the side you just beaded so the necklace will be balanced. Tape off the end of the lower strand, and bead the inner strand in the same manner, remembering to catch it in the spacer bar.

9. Slip two crimp beads on the end of the cord. Slide on one side of necklace fastener. Put the cord back through both crimp beads, come back over one bead and through the other crimp bead one more time to securely lock in the cord. Gently crimp the beads with flat-ose pliers.

10. Untape other end of necklace and slide the beads toward the finished end to provide several inches of cord to work with. Slide on two crimp beads, the other part of the necklace fastener, and thread cord as before. Crimp the beads and cut both ends of cord off very close to the crimped beads.

QUARTZ FILIGREE CHOKER

Silver jig links and quartz beads make a beautiful combination. The links were flattened with a jewelry hammer to increase their stability and give them a finished look.

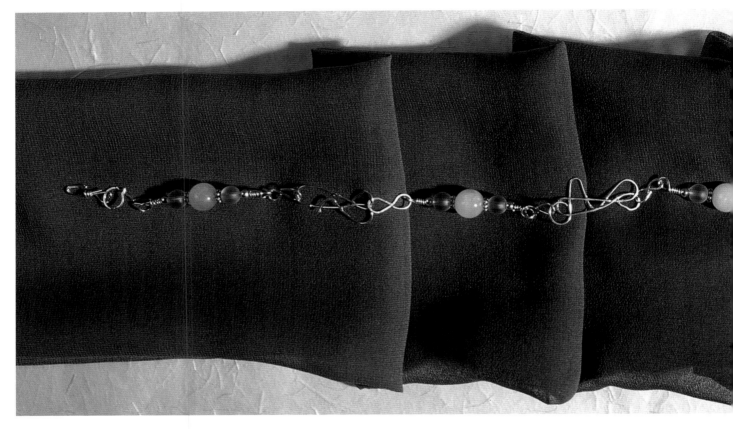

MATERIALS

- 5 8 mm rose quartz beads
- 10 6 mm rock quartz beads
- 10 silver spacers
- 10 silver seed beads
- 77-inch (1.96 m) length of 20-gauge silver wire
- Clasp findings

TOOLS

- Wire cutters
- Round-nose pliers
- Jig
- Soft mallet or jewelry hammer

INSTRUCTIONS

1. Cut five 6-inch (15 cm) lengths of wire. Onto each length slide one silver bead, one rock quartz bead, one spacer, one rose quartz bead, another spacer, another rock quartz bead, and another silver bead. Fold each end in a small loop and wrap the excess wire several times so that it butts against the silver bead.

2. Cut five 7-inch (17.5 cm) lengths of wire. Set up your jig, using the pattern in figure 9, page

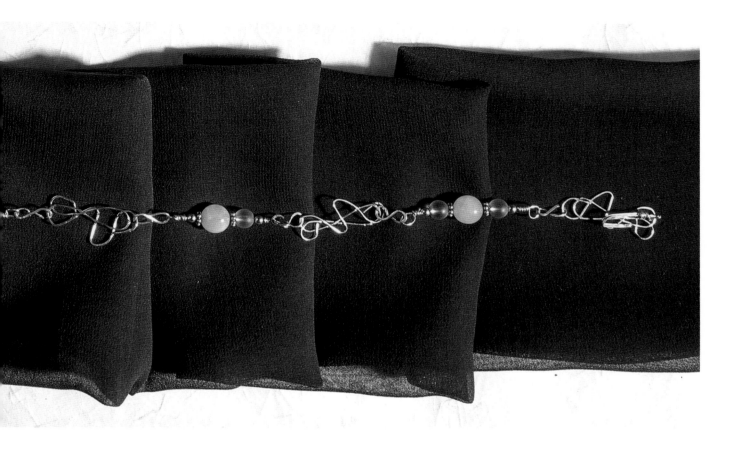

124 as a guide. To make each jig shape, make a large loop and wrap it around the top peg, then go to the left of the bottom peg, and go around the top peg.

3. Cut nine 1¼-inch (2.8 cm) lengths of wire and use the pliers to form figure-eight shapes with them by bending one end in a loop toward the middle from the right and the other end in a loop toward the middle from the left. Leave a small gap in the end of the loops. Cover the jig links with a soft cloth and flatten them with a soft mallet or jewelry hammer to increase their stability and to give them a finished look.

4. Use the figure-eight shapes to connect the bead and jig units. Gently try on the necklace and add additional figure eights at both ends of the necklace if extra length is desired. Close the gaps in the figure eights and add clasp findings.

DESIGNER: LILLI BRENNAN

GLASS BEAD NECKLACE AND EARRINGS

Don't limit yourself to single colors or patterns when choosing beads. The variety in this necklace is part of its appeal!

MATERIALS

- 18 8 mm glass beads
- 130-inch (3.3 m) length of 20-gauge wire

TOOLS

- Wire cutters
- Round-nose pliers
- Jig

INSTRUCTIONS

1. Cut 18 6-inch (15 cm) lengths of wire and make a small loop with the round-nose pliers on one end of each of them. Set up your jig, using the pattern in figure 10, page 125, as a guide.

2. Make a loop on a wire length and attach it to the jig's first peg. Wrap round the second and third pegs, then place a bead on the wire. Holding the bead tightly in place, continue wrapping around the fourth, fifth, and sixth pegs. Cut and remove the shaped wire from the jig.

3. Repeat step 2 with the remaining wire lengths. Tighten the wire around the beads by pulling on loops three and four with round-nose pliers until they're snug but not too tight. Flatten the wire around the beads so that the loops are centered on the bead.

4. Cut 17 1¼-inch (3.2 cm) lengths of wire and use the pliers to form figure-eight links with them by bending one end in a loop toward the middle from the right and the other end in a loop toward the middle from the left. Leave a small gap in the end of the loops.

5. Use the figure eights to connect all but two of the bead/jig links. Close the gaps in the figure eights with pliers and add clasp findings.

6. To make the earrings, attach a bead/jig link to each ear wire.

CAPTURED PEARLS BRACELETS

These bracelets use spool pegs to knit beads and wire together. Infinite variations can be created by varying the number of pegs, the color of the wire, the type of bead, etc. Finished bracelets can be twisted in one direction to accentuate the spiral effect or you can twist it in both directions and then straighten it to make the knitted loops appear thinner.

MATERIALS

- Spool of 24-gauge copper wire
- Strand of 4-8 mm freshwater pearls or semiprecious nuggets
- Copper bracelet findings
- 2 copper jump rings

TOOLS

- Wire cutters
- Knitting spool (commercially purchased or homemade replica)
- Steel crochet hook

INSTRUCTIONS

1. Thread the entire strand of beads onto the spool of wire. Do not cut the wire.

2. Drop about 6 inches (15 cm) of the wire down into the spool. Wind a loop around the first peg. Slide a bead between the first loop and the next peg (clockwise or counterclockwise, whichever is most comfortable for you).

3. Continue making loops and sliding beads as you work around the pegs until you're back at the first peg.

4. Make another loop on the first peg and bring the bottom loop over the peg with your crochet hook.

5. Repeat steps 3 and 4 until you're about an inch (2.5 cm) from your desired length. Tug on the length as it comes through the bottom of the spool when the peg area becomes too crowded.

6. Carefully lift the work off the pegs and slide it out of the spool. Cut the wire about 6 inches past the last bead. Take the working end of the wire and go through each loop at least once. (This step is the equivalent of casting off in knitting.)

7. Join a jump ring to each end of the bracelet using the wire as a sewing needle. Tuck in the wire ends and attach the findings.

DESIGNER: BARBARA VAN BUSKIRK

Gemstone Pendants

Commercially purchased gemstones can be transformed into fabulous pendants with just a handful of wire and some imagination. To form your own designs, simply trace your gemstone's shape on a piece of paper and sketch a variety of designs to find one you like.

Designer: R.P. Myers

MATERIALS

- 32-inch (81cm) length of 21-gauge, half-square, 14 k gold-filled wire
- 40 mm donut gemstone

TOOLS

- Wire cutters
- 1-inch (2.5 cm) dowel or steel rod
- Round-nose pliers
- Flat-nose pliers

1. Cut the wire into one 8-inch (20 cm) length and one 24-inch (61cm) length. Wrap the center of the 8-inch wire around the dowel twice to form a double loop for the bail. With the loops still on the dowel, cross the ends of the two wires and carefully twist them together as you would a twist-tie around a loaf of bread. Make two full twists.

2. Insert the end of the each wire into the center hole on opposite sides of the donut. Pulling each wire as tight as possible, bend the wires flat against the stone. With each wire lying across the face of the stone, cut them off where they meet the edge or center of the stone.

3. Carefully press the wires against the stone with flat-nose pliers. Using the round-nose pliers, twist each wire into loose rosettes as shown in the photo.

Using the flat-nose pliers, carefully grip the center of the wrap wires and twist them right or left. Tighten the wire around the stone and put a design in the wire.

4. Fold the 24-inch length of wire in half. Carefully insert the ends of the wire through the center hole from opposite sides of the stone. Holding the end of the wire with flat-nose pliers so you won't mar the wire, pull the wires tightly around the stone until they are pointing away from the stone's center. Reinsert the wires ends through the center hole, pulling them as tightly as possible and taking care to avoid kinks. Repeat step 3, then spread the bail wires as desired.

Motif Links Necklace, Earrings, & Bracelet

A medley of musical wire links combined with bead and square loop links creates a necklace that's sure to be noticed.

MATERIALS

- 14 6 mm beads
- 91-inch (2.31 m) length of 22-gauge gold wire
- 53-inch (1.35 m) length of 22-gauge green metal wire
- Clasp findings for the necklace and bracelet
- Post earring findings

TOOLS

- Wire cutters
- Round-nose pliers
- Jig

INSTRUCTIONS

1. Cut 14 1½-inch (4 cm) lengths from the gold wire. Form a loop around the round-nose pliers at one end of a length of wire. Slide on a bead and make a small loop close to the bead at the other end. Trim off any excess wire. Repeat with the remaining lengths of wire.

2. Cut eight 1¼-inch (3.2 cm) lengths from the gold wire and one from the green wire and form S-shaped links by curving one end of the wire in toward the center point around the round-nose pliers and then curving the other end in toward the center point in the opposite direction. Repeat with the remaining lengths of wire.

3. Cut nine 5½-inch (14 cm) lengths from the gold wire and two from the green wire. Set the jig in the pattern shown in figure 11 on page 125 and make 11 links. Trim any excess wire.

4. Cut nine 4½-inch (11.5 cm) lengths of green wire. Set the jig in the pattern shown in figure 12 on page 125 and make nine links.

5. Cut a 10½-inch (27 cm) length of gold wire. Reset the jig in the same pattern as in step 4 but with the pegs farther apart (2½ inches, 6 cm, apart at their farthest point) and make one link.

To Make the Necklace

1. Assemble the links in this order: one link from step 2, one link from step 3, another link from step 2, one link from step 4, a bead link, a link from step 3, another bead link, a link from step 4, another bead link, a link from step 3, another bead link, and a link from step 4. Repeat the series again to form a second chain.

2. Add a gold S-link from step 2 to each side of a link from step 3. Add the green S-link from step 2 to the top of the link from step 5, then attach it to the square link from step 3.

(Continued on page 65)

YOKE NECKLACE

A center yoke created from decorative wire loops forms the focal point for this simple necklace. Since only the center bead is showcased in this design, search out something special such as a handmade glass artist's bead.

MATERIALS

- 20-gauge gold wire
- Long focal bead
- 23 smaller, coordinating beads
- Head pin
- Clasp findings

TOOLS

- Wire cutters
- Round-nose pliers
- Jig

INSTRUCTIONS

1. Cut 22 pieces of wire to the length of your bead coordinating beads plus ⅝ inch (16 mm). Form a loop at one end of a length of wire. Slide on a bead so that it rests snugly against the loop. Form loop in the opposite direction at the other end close to the bead. Trim off any excess wire and repeat 21 times.

2. Arrange your jig pegs in a triangle shape that's a little wider than your bead. Add pegs in every hole along the two edges that come together in a point.

3. Make a loop on one end of a length of wire (length will vary depending on size of bead, but use at least an 8-inch, 20-cm, length). Start wrapping the wire at the center point peg and continue up the side. Slide the bead onto the wire and center within the space, then continue wrapping the remaining pegs.

3. Remove the wire from the jig and finger press to match up loop numbers 1 and 10.

4. Slide the remaining coordinating bead onto a head pin and form a loop close to the bead. Trim off any excess wire and attach the loop to the center, overlapping loops. Add clasp findings.

ICE BLUE NECKLACE

Simple bead links combine with alternating variations of the same jig pattern to create an enchanting piece. Make a few extra jig links for a matching bracelet and earrings.

MATERIALS

- 75½-inch (1.92 m) length of 20-gauge wire
- 14 glass beads
- Necklace clasp findings

TOOLS

- Wire cutters
- Round-nose pliers
- Jig
- Toothpick

INSTRUCTIONS

1. Cut the wire into seven 3½-inch (9 cm) lengths, six 5-inch (13 cm) lengths, and 14 1½-inch (3.8 cm) lengths.

2. Set up the jig as shown in the pattern in figure 13 on page 125. Wrap a length of 3½-inch wire around the pegs and then use a toothpick to push the link down between the pegs. Remove the link and repeat with the remaining 3½-inch wire lengths.

3. Add two pegs to the jig to form a three-loop shape. Wrap the 5-inch wire around the pegs and then use a toothpick to push the link down between the pegs. Remove the link and repeat with the remaining 5-inch wire lengths.

4. Make a loop on one end of a 1½-inch length of wire with round-nose pliers. Slide a bead onto the wire and against the loop. Form a second loop in the opposite direction close to the bead and trim off any excess wire. Repeat with the remaining 13 wire lengths.

5. Assemble the links, beginning with a bead link, then a two-loop jig link, then another bead link, then a three-loop jig link, and so on until you use up all of the links. Add clasp findings.

Bead and Wire Dragonflies

Many of the new colored wires are pliable enough to be easily bent into any number of creative shapes. Just be sure to choose lightweight beads to prevent shape distortion.

DESIGNER: SUSAN KINNEY

MATERIALS

- 24-inch (61 cm) length of 24- to 26-gauge colored wire
- 6 black seed beads for antennae
- 2 E beads for head
- 2 smaller darker beads for neck
- 2 slightly larger complementary beads with large holesfor body of dragonflies

TOOLS

- Wire cutters
- Round-nose pliers
- Small nail

INSTRUCTIONS

1. Cut the wire into two 12-inch (31 cm) lengths. Set one length aside.

2. Thread both ends of the wire through a head bead and neck bead, leaving an inch at the top.

3. Add three seed beads to each antennae. Coil the remaining wire around the nail to form curves.

4. Form wings by bending the wires around the nail and then twisting together. Thread a body bead on the ends of both wires and push up against first set of wings.

5. Repeat step 4 to make the lower set of wings. Twist the two wires tightly with your fingers to form the tail. Next, loop around the nail to form a small curl at the end of the tail.

(Instructions continued from page 58)

2. Add a gold S-link from step 2 to each side of a link from step 3. Add the green S-link from step 2 to the top of the link from step 5, then attach it to the center of the square link from step 3. Attach the gold s-links to the step 4 ends of the chains. Add clasp findings to each end. Check for loose connections and tighten as needed.

TO MAKE THE BRACELET

1. Assemble the links in this order: one gold S-shaped link from step 2, one green link from step 3, one bead link from step1, a gold link from step 3, another bead link, one link from step 4, another bead link, a gold link from step 3, another bead link, a green link from step 3, and a gold S-link from step 2. Add clasp findings to each end. Check for loose connections and tighten as needed.

TO MAKE EARRINGS

1. Cut two 5-inch lengths of green wire. Make a small bend ½ inch away from one end of the wire and form a coil around it that's at least large enough to cover the hole in the finding. Trim the second end of the wire to ¼ inch and form a small loop at the end. Note: Your loop should rest just below the earring finding, so trim off any excess wire before making the loop if necessary. Attach a bead link from step 1 to the loop hanging below the finding, then attach a link from step 4 to the bead link. Insert the wire protruding from the coil through the center of the earring finding. Try the earring on and attach the back finding. If the protruding wire is too long, trim off the excess. Repeat steps 1-3 to make the second earring.

WIRE SCROLL NECKLACE

Designer Mami Laher often uses large stone beads as the centerpiece of her bead and wire jewelry. She didn't have a large black bead on hand when designing this necklace, so she designed a wire scroll pendant to fill its place.

MATERIALS

- 1-foot (.9 m) length of 18-gauge round wire
- 6-foot (5.4 m) length of 20-gauge square wire
- 2-foot (1.8 m) length of 24-gauge square wire
- 6 6 mm silver-colored beads
- 8 7 mm faceted beads
- 4 8 mm faceted beads
- 2 9 mm faceted beads
- 2 10 mm faceted beads
- 8 mm focal bead
- 2 dozen 4 mm jump rings
- Clasp finding

TOOLS

- Wire cutters
- Pin vise
- Round-nose pliers
- Chain-nose pliers
- Flush cutters
- Emery board

DESIGNER: MAMI LAHER

INSTRUCTIONS

1. Cut four 14-inch (35 cm) lengths of 20-gauge wire and twist each one separately in a pin vise.

2. Form swirls on one end of a 2-inch (5 cm) length of twisted wire. Slide on a 6 mm bead, then swirl the other end of the wire in the opposite direction. Repeat with one more 6 mm bead and four 6 mm beads.

3. Repeat step 2 to make two scroll links from 2-inch lengths of untwisted 20-gauge wire and 6 mm beads. Repeat step 2 again to make two swirl links from 3-inch (7.5 cm) lengths of untwisted 20-gauge wire and 8 mm beads. Repeat step 2 again to make two swirl links from 3-inch lengths of twisted wire and 9 mm beads.

4. Form a small loop at one end of a 1-inch (2.5 cm) length of 20-gauge untwisted wire. Slide on a 6 mm bead, then make a loop at the other end close to the bead. Trim off any excess wire. Repeat once with another 6 mm bead and once with the 8 mm focal bead.

5. Make swirls at both ends of four pieces of 2½-inch-long (6.5 cm) twisted wire.

6. Form a twisted wire loop/bead link (see page 16) with a 1¾-inch (4.5 cm) length of 18-gauge wire and two beads. Slide the beads to each end. Position two swirl links from step 5 on each side of the wire with the swirls facing away from the wire. Secure the swirls in place by wrapping around three times with 24-gauge wire. Cut the wire flush and file the edges. Repeat to form a second, identical link.

For Pendant

7. Make swirls on both ends of three 2½-inch lengths of twisted wire. Add a gentle curve to one of the lengths.

8. Form a loop at one end of a 3¼-inch (8.3 cm) length of 18-gauge untwisted wire. Slide on a 10 mm bead and form out-facing swirls to the bottom end. Repeat to form an identical link.

9. Secure the two links made in step 8 together with three wraps of 24-gauge wire. Position each uncurved swirl made in step 7 against the base of the triangle and secure just above the bottom swirl with three wraps of 24-gauge wire. Add the curved swirl link from step 7 to the top, reshaping if necessary, and secure in place just below the swirls with three wraps of 24-gauge wire.

10. Add the focal bead link made in step 4 to the curved swirl. Attach the links together with jump rings in an alternating pattern, referring to the photo as a guide. Attach the pendant with jump rings and add a clasp.

MAKING A SWIRL

Hold the very end of the wire in the jaws of round-nose pliers. Use the tip of the jaws to make the smallest possible circle. Hold the wire in your left hand about 1½ inches from the pliers, then turn your right wrist in a counterclockwise direction while holding the pliers. Release pressure on the pliers and slide the jaw back around the partially completed circle. Hold and turn as you did before; repeat until you have a perfect circle. Hold the circle in place with chain-nose pliers and slowly turn your wrist counterclockwise to form a coil around the circle.

ANGEL WINGS NECKLACE

The intricate design in this piece is actually quite simple to achieve—just make the basic links and attach them in a pattern with jump rings.

MATERIALS

- 35-inch (89 cm) length of 18- or 20-gauge wire
- 8 x 20 mm crystal drop
- 8 to 10 mm round crystal bead
- Purchased chain
- 15 jump rings
- Clasp finding

TOOLS

- Wire cutters
- Round-nose pliers
- Chain-nose pliers
- Jig

INSTRUCTIONS

1. Cut a 5-inch (12.5 cm) length of wire. Arrange the jig as shown in figure 14 on page 125.

2. Form the first half of the drop link by bending the wire around the jig. Add the crystal drop to the wire, then bend the second half of the drop link. Trim off any excess wire.

3. Cut two 6-inch (15 cm) lengths of wire and make mirror image links by bending the wire as shown in the jig pattern in figure 15 on page 125. (Make mirror image links by wrapping the wire once in the direction shown in the figure and once in the opposite direction.)

4. Cut two 5½-inch (14 cm) lengths of wire and make mirror image links by bending the wire as shown in figure 16 on page 125.

5. Cut a 1¼-inch length (3.2 cm) of wire. Form a loop on one end with round-nose pliers. Slide the bead onto the wire and against the loop. Form a second loop at the other end of the wire in the opposite direction and trim off any excess wire.

6. Connect the ends of the loops with jump rings at the points indicated in figure 1. The open ends of each link should tug gently on each jump ring. If they don't, adjust the tension with round-nose pliers in the loop opposite the corner of each link.

7. Connect the links with jump rings as indicated in figure 2. Connect the points of each wing with one end of chain, then add a clasp.

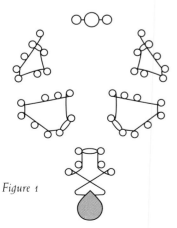

Figure 1

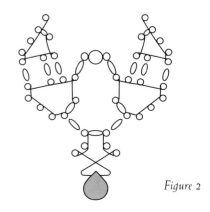

Figure 2

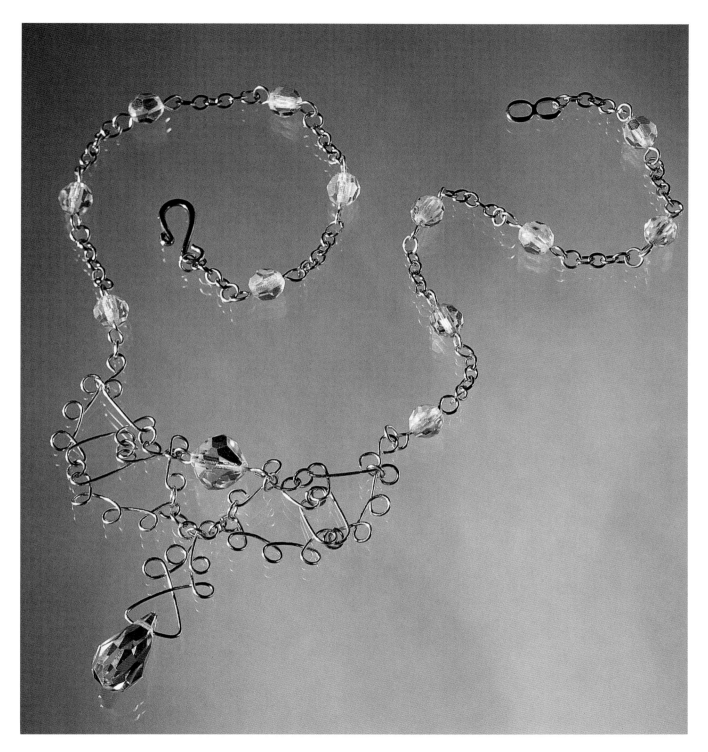

Dancing Bead People

Everyone will marvel at the personalities of these bead and wire people. Although you can follow these instructions step by step and create exact replicas, it's also fun to sift through your bead collection and let your favorite beads inspire new designs.

MATERIALS

For Earrings

- 56-inch (1.42 m) length of 26-gauge gold wire
- 14 Japanese matte beads (4 E beads for the feet, 6 E beads for the hands and hat, and 4 cylinder beads for the legs)
- 2 flat gold beads for the collar
- Gold earring wires

MATERIALS

For Pins or Pendants

- 49-inch (1.25 cm) length of 24- or 26-gauge colored wire
- 2 larger beads for head and body
- 4 smaller beads for feet and hands
- 2-3 dozen seed beads for legs (optional)
- Flat bead for neck (optional)
- Pin backing (for pin) or jump ring (for pendant)

TOOLS

- Wire cutters
- Small nail
- Round-nose pliers

INSTRUCTIONS

For Earrings (top)

1. Cut the wire into two 26-inch (66 cm) lengths. Holding the 24-inch wires together, fold them in half. Create the desired hairstyle by coiling the center of the wire around a nail.

2. Choose an interesting bead for the head and thread all four wires through. Add a flat gold bead to create the collar.

3. Bend the two wires at right angles and string on a hand bead. Twist the wire using your fingers and pliers until you get to the hand bead. Bend the arms into an interesting shape.

4. Thread the remaining two wires through a large bead for the body and push up against the arms. Add a fat bead for the body.

5. Thread the leg wires through the body bead and add a cylinder bead for each leg and an E bead for the feet. Coil a small curl to hold the bead on.

6. Open the earring's loop and attach it to the hair. Close the loop.

INSTRUCTIONS

For Pins or Pendants (bottom)

1. Cut the wire into two 24-inch (61 cm) lengths and one 1-inch (2.5 cm) length. Holding the wires together, fold them in half. Shape the desired hairstyle by coiling the center of the wire around a nail.

2. Repeat steps 2-6 above, using the 1-inch wire length to attach the pin backing; for a pendant, attach a jump ring in the hair.

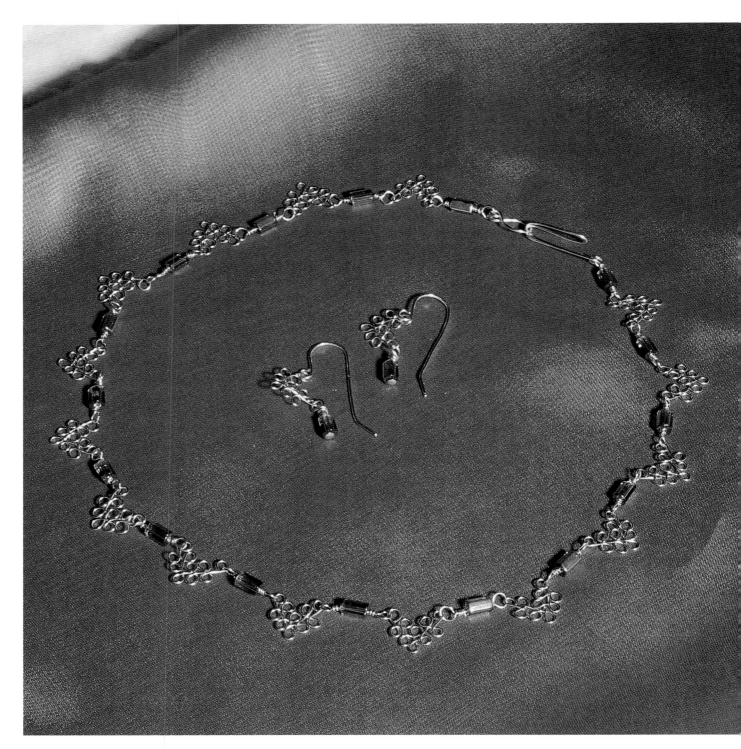

DESIGNER: LILLI BRENNAN

FILIGREE NECKLACE AND EARRINGS

A thin-gauge wire wrapped around a multiple-peg jig pattern creates lacy links that are simple to assemble into earrings, bracelets, and necklaces.

MATERIALS

- 63-inch (1.6 m) length of 22-gauge gold wire
- 18 6 mm amber tube beads
- Clasp findings
- Earring wires
- 2 head pins

TOOLS

- Wire cutters
- Jig
- Toothpick

INSTRUCTIONS

1. Cut the wire into 17 2½-inch lengths and 16 1¼-inch (3.8 cm) lengths. Note: This will make a 21-inch (53 cm) necklace; make additional links if a longer necklace is desired.

2. Set up the jig as shown in the pattern in figure 17 on page 125. Wrap the wire around the pegs and then use a toothpick to push the link down between the pegs. Repeat with the remaining 2½-inch wire lengths.

3. Bend a loop around the round-nose pliers about ¼ inch (3 mm) away from one end of a 1¼-inch length of wire. Wrap the wire two to three times at the base of the loop. Slide on a bead and make a loop and wraps at the other end. Trim off any excess wire. Repeat with the remaining lengths of 1¼-inch wire.

TO MAKE THE NECKLACE

4. Attach the jig and bead links together by sliding the loops in the bead links inside the ending loops in the jig links. (Reserve two jig links for the earrings.) Attach clasp findings at both ends.

TO MAKE THE EARRINGS

5. Slide a bead down the head pin and make a loop about ¼ inch (3 mm) away from the bead with round-nose pliers. Wrap the wire two to three times and trim off any excess wire.

6. Attach the bead's loop to the outermost loop in the jig link, then attach the jig link at the other end to an ear wire.

7. Repeat steps 5 and 6 for the second earring but position the jig link in the opposite direction.w

CLEOPATRA'S CHOKER

This inspiration for this piece came from photos of temple jewelry from the Egyptian pyramids, and, in turn, the design led to the development of two specialty jigs made by the WigJig company. The bead links are formed with a very thin gauge wire, which makes them seem to float in place when positioned next to the heavier gauge tree links.

DESIGNER: GARY HELWIG

MATERIALS

- Inexpensive practice wire
- 148-inch (3.76 m) length of 16-gauge half-hard wire
- 35-inch (89 cm) length of 22-gauge half-hard wire
- 10 mm black beads
- Necklace clasp finding

TOOLS

- Wire cutters
- Nylon pliers
- Round-nose pliers
- Jig

INSTRUCTIONS

1. Cut the practice wire into several 20-inch (51 cm) lengths. Set up your jig in the pattern shown in figure 18 on page 125. Loop a wire around the first peg, leaving a 5-inch (13 cm) tail at the top. Begin wrapping the wire in the pattern. Take extra care to make sure that the first two wraps have the same tension as the rest of the wraps. (The first two pegs are the most difficult; after you've wrapped them, they help hold the wire in place for subsequent wraps.)

2. Press the wrapped shape down on the jig and begin flattening the shape. Make spirals at the top and bottom of the shape, taking care to notice the direction of the wire. Trim off any excess wire. Harden the link into its finished shape with nylon pliers. Continue practicing until you are happy with the results.

3. Cut the 16-gauge wire into seven 20-inch lengths. Straighten the wire lengths by repeatedly pulling them through the jaws of the nylon pliers. Repeat steps 1 and 2 to make seven links, three of them left-facing and four of them right-facing.

4. Cut six 1¼-inch (3.2 cm) lengths from the remaining 16-gauge wire. Form figure-eight shapes by curving one end of the wire in toward the center point around the round-nose pliers and then curving the other end in toward the center point in the opposite direction. Repeat five times with the remaining wire.

5. Cut 20 1¾-inch (4.5 cm) lengths of 22-gauge wire. Form a small loop about ¼ inch (3 mm) away from one end. Begin connecting the tree links by slipping the top curves in the trees into the loop and then securing by making three wraps near the base of the loop. Slide on a bead, make another loop, and wrap again. Take care to place all of your left-facing and right-facing tree links next to each other.

6. Attach the trees together at their bases with the figure-eight links made in step 4.

7. Make two 7-bead chains and attach one on each side of the necklace. Add clasp findings.

Figure-Eight Bracelets

The figure-eight wire links that form the backbones of these bracelets (and matching earrings on page 79) create a strong, durable piece of jewelry that makes them ideal for everyday wear. Although these bracelets were all made with the same technique, their individual looks come from the variances in the bead links. You can also create different looks by changing the space between pegs and/or changing the wire gauge—just have enough extra materials on hand to allow for several practice links.

MATERIALS

- 30-inch (76 cm) length of 22-gauge wire plus extra wire for practice links
- 5 medium-size beads or 10 smaller size beads
- Clasp findings

TOOLS

- Wire cutters
- Round-nose pliers
- Jig

INSTRUCTIONS

1. Cut the wire into 10 3-inch (7.5 cm) lengths.

2. Make five bead links by forming a loop with one length of wire around the round-nose pliers, then sliding the bead down against the loop and making a second loop close to the bead. Trim any excess wire. Set the bead links aside.

3. To make a figure-eight link, position two large jig pegs ¼ to 3⁄16 inch (5 mm) apart. Tightly wrap a length of wire around the pegs in a figure-eight shape, leaving a ¾-inch (9 mm) tail at each end of the wire. Remove the figure eight from the jig by grasping it at the center point with round-nosed pliers. Repeat step 3 four more times.

4. Connect the bead links to the figure-eight links by slipping the bead links' loops onto the loops in the figure eights.

5. Finish the figure-eight links by bending the wire tails so they are perpendicular to the link. Hold the link in the middle with round-nose pliers and wrap the wire tails around the piece as shown in the illustration. Note that the wire from the right-hand loop forms the left-hand wrap around the center of the link, while the wire from the left-hand loop forms the right-hand wrap.

6. Place the bracelet on the intended wearer's arm and see if additional links are necessary.

7. Add clasp findings.

DESIGNER: GARY HELWIG

Figure-Eight Earrings

These earrings are a simple variation of the bracelets on page 76. Changing the size and distance between the pegs creates a figure-eight link small enough for earrings.

MATERIALS

- 6-inch (15 cm) length of 22-gauge wire plus extra wire for practice links
- 2 medium-size beads or 4 smaller size beads
- 2 head pins
- 2 2 mm gold beads
- Ear wires

TOOLS

- Wire cutters
- Round-nose pliers
- Jig

INSTRUCTIONS

1. Cut the wire into two 3-inch (7.5 cm) lengths.

2. Make a figure-eight link by positioning two jig pegs $\frac{3}{16}$ to $\frac{1}{4}$ inch (5 to 6 mm) apart. Tightly wrap a length of wire around the pegs in a figure-eight shape, leaving a $\frac{3}{4}$-inch (20 mm) tail at each end of the wire. Remove the figure eight from the jig by grasping it at the center point with round-nosed pliers. Repeat with the second wire.

3. Slide your focal bead(s) down the head pin and follow with a 2 mm bead. Form a small loop around the round-nose pliers close to the 2 mm bead. Connect the bead links to the figure-eight links by slipping the head pin loop onto one loop in the figure eights, then slip the ear wire loop onto the other loop in the figure eight. Repeat with the remaining head pin and beads.

4. Finish the figure-eight links by bending the wire tails so they are perpendicular to the link. Hold the link in the middle with round-nose pliers and wrap the wire tails around the piece as shown in Figure 1. Note that the wire from the right-hand loop forms the left-hand wrap around the center of the link, while the wire from the left-hand loop forms the right-hand wrap. Trim any excess wire.

DESIGNER: GARY HELWIG

Brass and Black Wire Bead Necklace

This necklace uses the same simple wire beadmaking techniques as the necklace on page 94, but the metallic color scheme gives it a totally different look.

Designer: Chris Gluck

MATERIALS

- 50 multicolored E beads
- 30 black spacer discs in sizes that complement your beads
- 36-inch (91.5 cm) length of beading cord
- Mixed assortment (approximately 22) of large beads
- 20-foot (6.1 m) length of gold plastic-coated wire
- 20-foot length of black plastic-coated wire

TOOLS

- Wire cutters or nail clippers
- ⅛-inch (3 mm) wood dowel, 6 inches (15 cm) long
- Slim popsicle stick
- Toothpick

* **Safety Note**: Some plastic-coated wire may contain lead. Get your wire from a professional supplier and verify that it does not contain lead before using.

INSTRUCTIONS

1. Use the plastic wire to make an assortment of wire beads in different lengths, colors, and shapes. (See Making Wire Beads, below.) The necklace shown here uses three double-coil beads, four spiral-coil beads, and two bead loop links.

2. String the beads onto the beading cord in an attractive pattern and hide your knot within a coil.

MAKING WIRE BEADS

- To make a spiral-coil bead, wrap a 2-foot (1.8 m) length of wire onto a popsicle stick. Press firmly all around, then pull off. (Do not pull too hard or it will be more difficult to remove.) The bead will spiral automatically; if it doesn't, form the twists by hand after you remove it from the stick.

- To make the E-bead loop coils, wrap a 2-foot length of wire five times around a ⅛-inch dowel at one end of the wire. Slide on ten small beads, then wrap the wire again five times. Trim off any excess wire.

- To make a double-wrapped coil bead, wrap a 2-foot length of wire around a toothpick or a length of 22-gauge wire. Repeat with a second 2-foot length of wire, then wrap this coil around a ⅛-inch dowel to create a coiled coil. Trim the coiled coil to the desired length, then string it over a length of single coil just a little longer than the desired bead length.

- To make a crimped bead, feed two 2-foot lengths of wire in contrasting colors through a paper crimper, then wrap them carefully side by side on a ⅛-inch dowel until you have used up all of the wire. Cut the crimped wire into beads of the desired length and string them over a length of single coil (done over a toothpick or length of 22-gauge wire) that's just a little longer than the crimped bead.

Handcrafted Bead Pendants

Designer: R.P. Myers; Glass Artists: Michael Barley (left) and Bill Glass (right)

MATERIALS

For Pendant at Left

- 4-foot (3.6 m) length of 21-gauge, dead-soft, square 14K gold-filled wire
- 6-inch (15 cm) length of 21-gauge half-square or round 14K gold-filled wire
- 8-inch (20 cm) length of 20-gauge half-round 14K gold-filled wire
- 6-inch length of 24-gauge hard square or round 14K gold-filled wire
- 7 5 or 6 mm pearls

TOOLS

- Wire cutters
- Pin vise
- Round-, flat-, and chain-nose pliers

MATERIALS

- 28-inch (71 cm) length of 18-gauge, dead-soft square 14K gold-filled wire
- 16-inch (41 cm) length of 21-gauge, dead-soft square 14K gold-filled wire
- 8-inch (20 cm) length of 18-gauge, hard round 14K gold-filled wire
- Large fused glass bead

TOOLS

- Wire cutters
- Pin vise
- Round-, flat, and chain-nose pliers
- 1/8-inch-wide (3 mm) metal rod or wood dowel

INSTRUCTIONS

For Pedant at Left

1. Cut the 21-gauge dead-soft wire into three 14-inch (35 cm) lengths. Twist two of the lengths together in a pin vise. Hold the twisted and untwisted wires together and mark their halfway point. Measure the length of the bead and move down the wire half of this distance. Make two wire wraps at this point with the 20-gauge wire. Slip the bead over the unwrapped side of the bundle and make two wraps with the 20-gauge wire at the other end of the bead.

2. Carefully curl the wires on one side of the bead into a complete circle, then continue past the point where they come together for another 90 degrees. Repeat on the other side. Visualize an imaginary line running vertically through the center of the bead. Pull a twisted wire from each side of the bead together about an inch above the top of the bead. Bend the wires where they cross until they are parallel to each other along your imaginary line.

3. Place your round-nose pliers perpendicular to the parallel wires, and roll the wires forward until they lie down the center of the bead, forming the bail. Press the wires together so that all four are parallel about ⅜ inch down from the top of the bail. Bend an offset hook deep enough to go over all four wires at one end of the 20-gauge wire. Wrap the wire around all four bail wires, beginning at the point where the two wires come together from the bead. Continue wrapping until you reach the point where the wires separate to form the bail. Secure the ends of the 20-gauge wire by squeezing flat and smooth with chain-nose pliers.

4. Carefully pull the remaining four wires across the wire harness until they form a woven pattern as seen in the photo. When the desired placement is achieved, cut off the excess wire, leaving just enough length to securely wrap around the harness wires. Form a 360-degree loop at the center of the 6-inch length of half-hard square wire. Form a loop the same size as the center loop on each side, spacing the loops as looks best with the bead. With the loops facing down, bend the ends of the wire up equally distant from the center loop so that the distance between the vertical bends is 1/16 inch wider than the bead is long. Form an eye loop on each vertical wire that's large enough to go over the binding wires of the main bead harness. Open the eye loops and hang the loop wire on each side of the bead as seen in the photo.

5. Cut the 24-gauge wire into three equal lengths. Make a small loop at one end of each wire. Drop two pearls onto two wires and three onto the remaining wire. Attach the pearls to the pendant by looping the wire ends through the loops made in the pendant.

INSTRUCTIONS

For Pendant at Right

1. Cut the 21-gauge wire in half, then twist them plus the 28-inch length of wire separately in the pin vise. Mark the center of the 28-inch wire and move down the wire from this point half the distance of the bead's width. Curl the wire on one side of the bead into a complete circle, then continue past the point where they come together for another 90 degrees. Slip the bead onto the wire so that it rests against the curl, then repeat on the other side.

2. Visualize an imaginary line running vertically through the center of the bead. Pull a twisted wire from each side of the bead together about an inch above the top of the bead. Bend the wires where they cross until they are parallel to each other along your imaginary line.

(Continued on page 95)

GEISHA GIRL EARRINGS

These playful earrings are as much fun to make as they are to wear. Make a half dozen pairs in different color patterns and keep them on hand for special gift-giving occasions.

DESIGNER: SHARON BATEMAN

MATERIALS

- 44½ inches (1.13 m) 20-gauge wire
- 2 6 mm round beads
- 2 8-12 mm cupped flower beads
- 2 small (4 mm or size 6/0 or 8/0) drops
- 2 10/0 seed beads or drops
- Delica seed beads in two or more colors
- Ear wires

TOOLS

- Wire cutters
- Round-nose pliers
- Flat-nose pliers

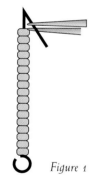

Figure 1

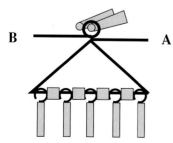

Figure 2

INSTRUCTIONS

1. Cut the wire into the following lengths: two 4-inch (10 cm) lengths for the body, 12 1½-inch (4 cm) lengths for the sleeves, six 1¾-inch (4.5 cm) lengths for the skirt, and four 2-inch (5 cm) lengths for the legs.

2. Bend ¼ inch (3 mm) of one end of each wire so that it's at a 90-degree angle to the rest of the length. Place your round-nose pliers at the end of the ¼-inch bend and bend the wire up and over them to form a loop. Note: If your loop does not close, make your 90-degree bends slightly larger than ¼ inch; if the loop has too much wire, make the 90-degree bends with slightly less wire.

3. Slip the delica beads onto each wire, using 12 beads for each sleeve and 17 beads for the skirt and legs.

4. Bend the wire down at a 45-degree angle, leaving a gap on the wire that is the length of one bead. Cut the excess wire slightly shorter than one bead length. Pinch the bend closed with flat-nosed pliers so that it resembles one end of a staple.

5. Bend the body wire at a 45-degree angle 1½ inches from one end. Slide the loops of the beaded skirt and leg wires onto the body wire, placing a single delica bead between them.

6. Bend the other end of the wire up and across so that it crosses the first bend. Bend wire end A up so that it is perpendicular to the skirt, then bend the wire end B to the left and around A twice.

7. Fold A over to the right and B to the left around round-nose pliers to form a loop. Slide four Delica beads onto wire A. Slide the loops of the sleeves on next, adding a bead between them. Add the white bead for the hand and work a staple bend at the end as you did in step 4. Repeat on the other side.

8. To form the head, add a head bead and a black flower bead. Work a loop with the round-nose pliers and slide the beads up to the loop. Cut the wire ¼ inch away from the bead and bend the other end into a loop without fully closing it. Attach the head section onto the body loop and close the loop. Add ear wires to the top loop of the head section. Repeat to form a second earring.

INSTRUCTIONS

Note: The instructions for both bracelets are the same until step 7.

1. Place one end of the 15-inch length of wire in the vise and straighten by pulling the polishing cloth down the length of the wire several times.

2. Place the 6½-inch length of wire in the vise ¼ inch (3 mm) and grasp it with the flat-nose pliers ¼ inch from the other end. Twist until you have a nice, even, fine pattern and leave the ends untwisted.

3. Bend the 15-inch length of wire in half using the round-nose pliers, making a loop about half the way up the pliers. Add the twisted wire to the middle of the 15-inch wire, holding ¼ inch in from the loop end. Wrap tape around the wire bundle about 2 inches (5 cm) and 5 inches (13 cm) from the loop to prevent the wires from twisting as you wrap them.

4. Using the 10-inch wire, make an angled bend at the end of the flat-nose pliers. Hook the bend over the bundle ½ inch from the loop (¼ inch from the twisted wire end). Grasp the hook and wire bundle with the flat-nose pliers and firmly wrap the half-round wire around the bundle five times, keeping the bundle straight and ending in the back. Snip the half-round wire and bevel-file with the emery board, then press it against the wire.

5. Grasp the end of the twisted wire and bend back over the inside of your first wrap. As you work, bend the tip of the wire down, then press against the wrap to secure the end of the twisted wire.

6. Add two more wire wraps about 1 inch apart. You should have one wrap about ½ inch from the ends, one wrap close to each side of the bead area, and one wrap centered between the end and the bead wrap.

7. At this point you are about 3 inches (7.5 cm) into the project. Remove the tape on the 5-inch mark. Slightly bend out the outer wires and slide your beads along the center twisted wire. Check and center the beads, then pull the wire bundle snug around them. You may wish to use round- or flat-nose pliers to help you make a symmetrical bend around the beads, depending on their shape. To make the fused glass bracelet, rout the glass according to the instructions on page 33, then run the twisted center wire over, under, or through the bead hole depending on your preference.

8. Tape the wire bundle in two places again to hold the wires straight. Wire wrap next to the beads to hold them tight. Center the next wire wrap between the bead wrap and the end wrap. The end wrap should be ¼ inch in from the end of the twisted wire.

9. Bend the twisted wire back over the bundle as in step 5. About ½ inch of wire should remain at the end. Pinch these together with the flat-nose pliers and snip to even. File the edge square, then grasp with round-nose pliers and bend the wire into a J shape to form the clasp.

10. Shape the bracelet to form an oval by grasping the ends and slowly bending them toward each other as you brace the middle against a table. Use your fingers to keep tension on the whole piece so that it doesn't kink.

The style of these wire-wrapped bracelets (and the ones on page 34) was inspired by some of the designer's rock-hound friends.

MATERIALS

- 15-inch (38 cm) length of 21-gauge gold-filled, half-hard square wire or 21-gauge full-hard square silver wire

- 6½-inch (16.5 cm) length of 20-gauge gold-filled, dead-soft square wire or 18-gauge dead-soft square silver wire

- 10-inch (25 cm) length of 21-gauge gold-filled, half-round wire or 21-gauge half-round silver wire

- Gold dichroic bead and 2 4 mm topaz beads for upright bracelet or rectangular fused glass disk or bead for flush bracelet

* Note: These wire lengths will make a 7-inch (18 cm) bracelet; allow extra wire for larger sizes.

TOOLS

- Pin vise or c-clamp

- Flat- and roundnose pliers

- Wire cutters

- Tape & emery board

- Polishing cloth

DESIGNER & BEAD ARTIST: GERI OMOHUNDRO

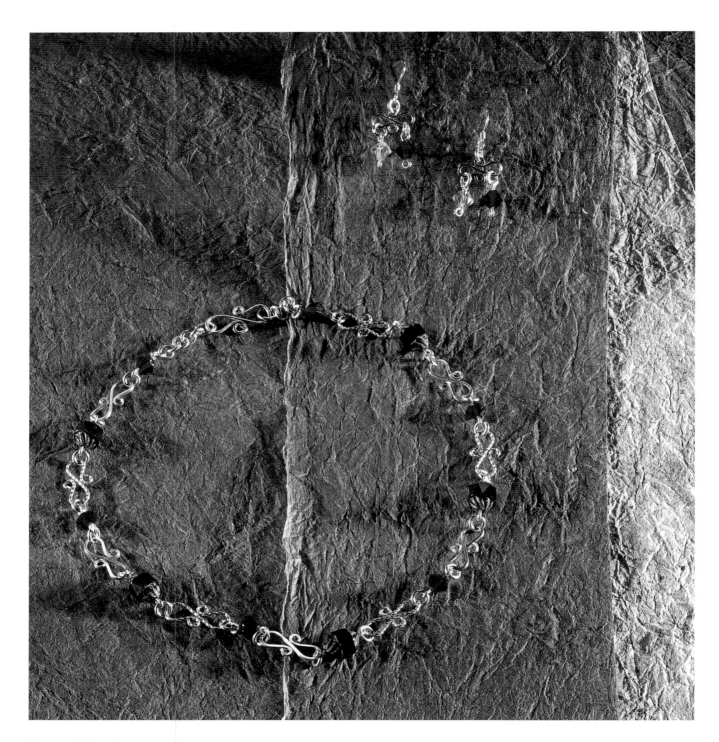

DESIGNER: MAMI LAHER

FACETED BEADS NECKLACE & EARRINGS

The designer of this necklace chose a simple design that fits close to the neck to draw attention to the faceted Austrian crystal beads.

MATERIALS

- 3-foot (2.7 m) length of 20-gauge square wire
- 5 10 mm faceted red beads
- 8 5 mm faceted red beads
- 2 5 mm faceted crystal beads
- 4 dozen 4 mm jump rings
- 2 6 mm jump rings
- Ear wires

TOOLS

- Wire cutters
- Round-nose pliers
- Chain-nose pliers
- Flush cutters
- Pin vise

INSTRUCTIONS

1. Cut the wire into one 14-inch (36 cm) length, eight 2-inch (4 cm) lengths, and 15 1-inch (2.5 cm) lengths.

2. Put the ends of the 14-inch wire length into the pin vise and twist. Cut the twisted wire into 2-inch lengths.

3. Make a loop on one end of an untwisted 2-inch wire length using the very tip of the round-nose pliers. Do the same at the other end, but face the loop in the opposite direction. Repeat on the remaining untwisted and twisted 2-inch wire lengths. Set aside one untwisted link for the clasp and two untwisted links for the earrings.

4. Make a loop at the end of each 1-inch wire length around round-nose pliers. Slide on a bead, then make another loop close to the bead at the other end. Trim off any excess wire. Set two 5 mm red bead links and two 5 mm crystal links aside for the earrings.

5. Attach the links together using jump rings, alternating between twisted and untwisted wire links and 6- and 8-mm bead links.

6. Add several 4 mm jump rings to the last link on each end. (Seven rings were used on each side here; add more or less to customize the fit.) Attach a 6 mm jump ring to each side.

7. Attach the link reserved for a clasp in step 3 to one of the 6 mm jump rings. Gently separate one side off the link reserved enough to allow the other 6 mm jump ring to slide on and off easily.

To Make the Earrings

8. Attach a jump ring to the top loop of one of the links made in step 3 and attach the jump ring to the earring. Repeat for the other earring. Attach a jump ring to each of the 5 mm bead links made in step 4. Attach a crystal bead link to one side of the link and a red bead link to the other side. Repeat for the other earring.

Bead Flower Choker and Earrings

This design is surprisingly simple to create—just make the bead flower links with a jig and attach them with jump rings. For variation, alternate bead and/or wire colors within the same piece, or add additional units to create longer necklaces or bracelets.

INSTRUCTIONS

1. Cut 31 5½-inch (14 cm) wire lengths, 27 for the choker and one for each earring. Cut additional lengths for more necklace length if desired.

2. Make a loop on one end of each length of wire and add a bead. Set up the jig as directed in figure 19 on page 124. Follow the jig shape with all but two pieces of the wire. When finished each unit should have a bead in the center that sits on the top of the right side. (The bead will be recessed on the wrong side.)

3. Set up the jig as directed in figure 5 on page 124. Make two links from the remaining two 5-1/2-inch lengths of wire.

4. Attach all but two of the jig shapes made in step 2 with jump rings, taking care that all of the units are facing right side up.

5. Attach clasp findings at each end to the links made in step 3, then attach these links to each end of the choker.

6. To make the earrings, attach a jig shape from step 2 to each ear wire. Drop a bead onto each head pin and attach the head pin to the bottom center of the jig shape.

MATERIALS

- 171-inch (4.34 m) length of 24-gauge wire
- 31 4 mm round beads
- 26 3 mm jump rings
- Claspfindings•
- 2 head pins
- Earring wires

TOOLS

- Wire cutters
- Round-nose pliers
- Jig

DESIGNER: LILLI BRENNAN

INSTRUCTIONS

1. Cut the 22-gauge wire into 13 1¼-inch (4.5 cm) lengths. Make a loop around the round-nose pliers about ½ inch (13 mm) away from one end and wrap the end wire around three times at the base of the loop. Slide on an 8 mm bead and form a loop and wraps at the other end that rests flush against the bead. Trim off any excess wire. Repeat with all of the remaining 8 mm beads and all but one (the thicker one) of the remaining heart-shaped beads.

2. Cut eight 1¼-inch lengths from the 14-gauge wire and form figure-eight-shaped links by curving one end of the wire in toward the center point around the round-nose pliers and then curving the other end in toward the center point in the opposite direction. Repeat seven times with the remaining wire.

3. Cut four 3½-inch (9 cm) lengths from the 14-gauge wire and form links by repeating step 2, but this time curving the wire into to a point about ⅛ inch (1.5 mm) away from the center.

4. Cut six 4¼-inch (11 cm) lengths from the 14-gauge wire and use the jig pattern in figure 20 on page 126 to form links. Trim off any excess wire.

5. Cut four 4¼-inch lengths from the 14-gauge wire and use the jig pattern in figure 21 on page 126 to form links. Trim off any excess wire.

6. Cut a 15-inch (38 cm) length of 14-gauge wire and use the jig pattern in figure 22 on page 126 to form the flower shape. Cut a 2-inch (5 cm) length of 22-gauge wire and thread it through the remaining heart-shaped bead, then secure the bead to the center of the flower with several wraps around the wire petals on the back side. Trim off any excess wire.

7. Assemble the links in this order: four S-shaped links from step 2, one link from step 4, one 8 mm bead link, one link from step 3, one 8 mm bead link, another link from step 4, one heart-shaped bead link, one link from step 5, another heart-shaped bead link, another link from step 4, another 8 mm bead link, another link from step 3, another 8 mm bead link, and another link from step 5. Repeat the series again to form a second chain.

8. Cut a 2½-inch length of 14-gauge wire. Thread the remaining heart-shaped wire link onto the wire, then cross the wires at the center point. Form a loop at either end of the wire and attach the step 5 link end of each chain to the loop.

9. Slide the lower end of the heart-shaped link drop onto the loop at the top of the flower. Add clasp findings at the end of the necklace.

10. Check for loose connecting links and tighten as needed.

DESIGNER: KAREN RAY

Colored Wire Necklace

Substituting a heavier gauge of wire and faux marble beads for the popular thin wire/glass beads combination creates a totally different look.

Materials

- 8 8 mm beads
- 6 heart-shaped beads, one of them about twice as thick if possible
- 16¼-inch (41 cm) length of 22-gauge colored wire
- 84-inch (2.14 m) length of 14-gauge colored wire
- Clasp findings

Tools

- Wire cutters
- Round-nose pliers
- Jig

COLORFUL WIRE BEAD NECKLACE

Remember the thrill of finding leftover telephone wire and the fun you and your friends would have making jewelry from it when you were kids? Well, the fun of working with plastic-coated wire is still the same, but the results can be much, much better!

DESIGNER: CHRIS GLUCK

* **Safety Note:** Some plastic-coated wire may contain lead. Get your wire from a professional supplier and verify that it does not contain lead before using.

MATERIALS

- 14 square ceramic beads
- 70 multicolored AB E beads
- 22 black wood disc beads
- 10 blue round or oval glass beads
- 4 red triangle glass beads
- 36-inch (92 cm) length of beading cord
- 82 feet (2.1 m) plastic-coated wire*

TOOLS

- Wire cutters or nail clippers
- Paper crimper
- ⅛-inch (3 mm) wood dowel
- Slim popsicle stick
- Toothpick

INSTRUCTIONS

1. Use the plastic wire to make an assortment of wire beads in different lengths, colors, and shapes. (See Making Wire Beads, page 81.) The necklace shown here uses three double-coil beads, 10 spiral-coil beads, 16 crimped-coil beads, and four bead loop links.

2. Cut a piece of wire to 14 inches (30 cm) long. Make a loop at one end about ¼ inch (6 mm) away from the end. String on a square wood bead so that it rests securely against the knot. Make several twists and trim off any excess wire. String the remaining length of the wire with crimped beads using square black beads as spacers. (Remember to string the crimped beads over a length of wire coils about ¼ inch longer than the crimped bead.) Finish the second end as you did the first.

3. Tie one end of the stringing material onto the loop formed in step 2. Hide the knot under the square bead. String on the remaining beads in an attractive pattern, remembering to string the crimped and large coil beads over a length of wire coil about ¼ inch longer than the crimped beads.

(Continued from page 83)

3. Place your round-nose pliers perpendicular to the parallel wires, roll the wires forward until they lie down the center of the bead, forming the bail. Press the wires together so that all four are parallel about 3/8 inch down from the top of the bail. Bend an offset hook deep enough to go over all four wires at one end of the 20-gauge wire. Wrap the wire around all four bail wires, beginning at the point where the two wires come together from the bead. Continue wrapping until you reach the point where the wires separate to form the bail. Secure the ends of the 20-gauge wire by squeezing them flat and smooth with chain-nose pliers. Holding the binding very securely between your thumb and forefinger of one hand, curl the wires that are lying down the center of the bead into a swirl that nearly covers the binding wire. Sweep the remaining wires down to be tied off on one of the wires coming up from the bead. Trim the wires off about an inch beyond the point where they are to be tied off. Using chain-nose pliers, bend a hook at each wire end and crimp them snugly down on the main wires, taking care not to mar the wires. Form coils in each of the 8-inch lengths of twisted 21-gauge wire by wrapping them around the rod or dowel, beginning and ending about an inch down from each wire end. Form a tight swirl shape at one end of each coiled wire length, referring to the photo as a guide. Trim off any excess wire. Gently pull on the coils to spread them out in a spring-like shape. Hold them against the bead and trim off any excess wire, leaving just enough to form a hanging loop to attach them to the loops on either side of the bead.

MATERIALS

- 42½-inch (1.1 m) length of colored metal wire
- 4 large (20 mm long) chevrons
- 8 small (15 mm long) chevrons
- 27 8 mm crystal or glass beads

TOOLS

- Wire cutters
- Round-nose pliers
- Jig
- Needle-nose pliers
- Masking tape

1. Cut the wire into one 12-inch (31 cm) length, two 3¼-inch (8.25 cm) lengths, two 2-inch (5 cm) lengths, two 7½-inch (19 cm) lengths, and two 2½-inch (6.5 cm) lengths. Wrap both pairs of pliers in masking tape to protect the colored finish on the wire.

2. Slide five crystal beads onto the 12-inch wire length for the centerpiece. Arrange the jig pegs as shown in figure 23 on page 126. Wrap the wire around the jig, moving the beads as you wrap so that one beads ends up between each set of loops.

3. Pull the end loops of the wire around to loop together. Shape the wire with your fingers to form the centerpiece shown, referring to the photo as a guide.

4. Form a loop on one end of a 3¼-inch length of wire with the round-nose pliers. Attach the loop to the base of the large loop on the centerpiece at about the 2 o'clock position. Bend the loop so that it will lie flat as the centerpiece loops do.

5. Slide one crystal bead, a large chevron bead, and another crystal bead onto the wire from step 4. Form another flat loop at the other end and loop toward the back to create the area where the next section will attach.

6. Repeat steps 4 and 5 for the other side of the centerpiece. Form a flat loop at one end of a 2-inch length of wire and attach it to the section just created. Slide on a large chevron bead and form another flat loop. Repeat for the other side.

7. Form a small loop at one end of the 7½-inch length of wire. Wrap the wire around two to three times and then attach this piece to the section just completed. Slide the beads onto the wire in the following order: two crystals, one small chevron, two more crystals, another small chevron, two more crystals, another small chevron, two more crystals, another small chevron, and one crystal. Repeat step 8 for the other side.

8. Arrange the jig and wrap the wire as shown in the patterns shown in figure 5 on page 124 to form the hook and catch, then attach them to the looped ends.

DESIGNER: SHARON HEUSSON

BEAD & WIRE NECKLACE

This simple necklace uses the same techniques as most of the other projects in this book, but the bright colors, heavy-gauge wire, and large jig link help create a distinctively different look.

TURQUOISE STONE NECKLACE

An elaborate bead and wire centerpiece was attached to a simple, pur-chased chain to create this stunning piece.

DESIGNER: SHARON BATEMAN

MATERIALS

- 2- x 3-inch (5 x 7.5 cm) piece of stiff backing material
- 3-inch square of leather or synthetic suede
- 25 x 18 mm stone cab
- Epoxy
- Fabric glue
- 2 strands each of 11/0 seed beads
- Assortment of 8 to 10 mm beads
- 27-inch (69 cm) length of 18- or 20-gauge wire
- Beading thread
- Jump rings
- #12 beading needle
- Chain link necklace

TOOLS

- Wire cutters
- Round- and flat-nose pliers
- Jig
- Craft knife

INSTRUCTIONS

PREPARING THE CAB

1. Attach the stone cab to one corner of the backing material with epoxy or glue. Glue the leather to other side of the backing material. Place light-weight objects on top of them and set aside to dry.

2. Thread the needle and knot the thread. Run the needle up through the backing next to the cab. String on two beads and push them down to the backing material. Run the needle down through the backing and back up through between the beads just added. Run the needle through the second bead of the two just added. Repeat as needed around the bottom area of the cab, then add additional rows, referring to the photo as a guide. Begin a new row by running your needle down through the backing and back up to the next to the last bead of the previous row. Cut off any excess material around the beaded cab.

3. Place the cab face up on top of the leather/suede and trace around the edges with a pencil. Cut out the backing material along the penciled line.

4. Cut three 1-inch (2.5 cm) lengths of wire and use the round-nose pliers to make connecting loops on one end of each wire. (See figure 1.)

5. Dip one end of each connector unit into the expoxy and slip between the layers. Make sure the edges are neatly aligned. Allow the glue to completely dry. Glue the beaded cab onto the prepared back, positioning all of the edges so the corners match. Trim any uneven edges.

ADDING A BEADED BORDER

6. Run a knotted thread up through the top layers of the backing, hiding the knot at the edge of the backing. String on three seed beads and run the thread up through both layers of the backing. Run the thread through the backing and then back through the third bead.

7. String on two more seed beads, run the thread through all layers of the backing and then run the thread back through the second bead of the two just added. Continue adding beads around the cab in this way until you approach the end. String on the last bead and run the thread through the first bead of the edging, through the layers, and back up through the first bead. Knot the thread between the beads and tie off.

8. Cut two 5-inch (12.5 cm) lengths of wire and set up your jig according the figure 24 on page 99. Make a link from each wire, one in the direction shown on the jig and one starting in the opposite direction to form a perfect opposite.

(Continued on following page)

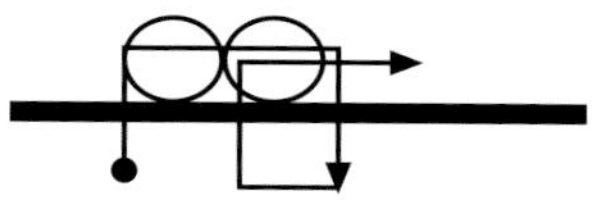

Figure 1

Figure 2

Figure 3

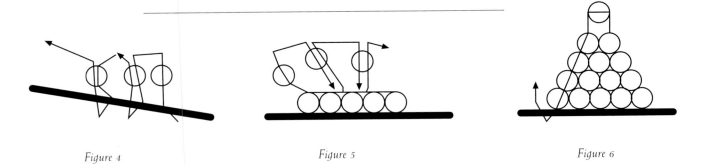

Figure 4

Figure 5

Figure 6

9. Cut two 12-inch (30 cm) wires. Bend a loop at one end of a wire with round-nose pliers. Pinch the loop with the flat-nosed pliers and curl the loop up to form a spiral. Repeat two or three more times, then make a matching spiral with the second wire. Do not cut the tails.

10. Set up your jig according to figure 25 on page 126. Make one link in the direction indicated with the spiral at the "start" end of the wire, positioning a ¼-inch (3 mm) peg in the hole indicated or holding a ¼-inch dowel in place. Make a second link by working the jig in the opposite direction. Push the circles that you wrapped three times slightly flat, making sure they lie in opposite directions. Cut two 1-inch lengths of wire and form a ¼-inch (3 mm) loop on one end around the round-nose pliers. Slide a bead down against each loop, then make a second loop in the opposite direction on the other end.

FILLING THE TRIANGLES WITH SEED BEADS

11. Tie a length of thread onto the wire. String on two beads. Run the needle under the wire and up through the second bead. (*) String on one bead. Run the needle under the wire and up through the bead just added. Repeat from (*) until you have the desired number of beads. (See figure 4.)

12. Begin each row by stringing on two beads. Run the needle under the second thread showing between the beads of the previous row. Run the thread back up through the second bead of the two just added (figure 5). (*) String on one bead. Run the needle under the next thread and back up through the bead just added. Repeat from (*) until there are no more threads to work on. Begin a new row.

13. Continue working rows until you reach the last row. (See figure 6.) String on two beads and run up through the last. String on one bead. Run the needle through the side beads of the triangle to the wire. Tie a knot at the base of the triangle and trim the thread

14. Repeat steps 11-13 on the remaining two triangles. Connect the links to the beaded cab, referring to figure 7 as a guide. Make a fifth link using complementary 8 to 10 mm beads and seed beads. Attach with a jump ring on the bottom connector. Add a chain with a clasps to the fourth link on each side of the cab.

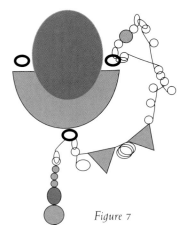

Figure 7

WIRE BEAD RINGS

Bead and wire rings are a great way to use up your favorite leftover beads. The rings slip easily onto any size finger (making them the ideal gift) and simply bend to close.

DESIGNER: LILLI BRENNAN

MATERIALS
- Length of 18-gauge wire the distance around your finger plus 2 inches (5 cm)
- 3 to 4 mm beads

TOOLS
- Wire cutters
- Round-nose pliers

INSTRUCTIONS

1. Make a small loop in one end of the wire with the round-nose pliers. Work the wire around the loop three times.

2. Slide the beads down all but the last inch of the wire.

3. Repeat step 1, working in the opposite direction.

GLASS BEAD EARRINGS

These earrings use the same basic techniques as those on pages 110 and 111, but the looks are completely different. Designer tip: "Work on both earrings at the same time to keep variations to a minimum."

- 10-inch (25 cm) length of 18-gauge sterling silver wire
- 2 small jump rings
- 2 ear wires
- 2 glass beads with openings wide enough for wire to fit through

MATERIALS

For Earrings at Bottom

- 10-inch (25 cm) length of 18-gauge sterling silver wire
- 2 square glass beads
- 2 jump rings
- 2-inch (5 cm) length of 20-gauge sterling silver wire

TOOLS

For Both Earrings

- Wire cutters
- Round-nose pliers

INSTRUCTIONS

For Earrings at Top

1. Cut the wire in half. Make a small loop on each end of the wire, following the natural curve of the wire. Make a second loop ¾ inch (9 mm) from the first loop. Make a loop in the end of the wire.

2. Slide a bead over the loop. Bring the two end loops together and overlap them around a pen or dowel to form an oval.

3. Connect the ear wire and the oval wire with a jump ring.

INSTRUCTIONS

For Earrings at Bottom

1. Cut both lengths of wire in half. Place the pliers in the center of the 18-gauge wire and bend slightly to form two sides of a triangle. Make another bend 1 inch (2.5 cm) in from the center on each side of the center. The wires should cross in the center.

2. Place the pliers where the wires cross. Bring the excess wire across the top of the pliers, crossing again. Trim the wires ⅜ inch (9 mm) from the crossing on each side. Form a loop on each end and overlap them.

3. Make a small coil on one end of the 20-gauge wire. Slide the bead down the wire until it rests on the coil. Trim the wire to ⅜ inch and make a loop. Attach the loop to the first crossover and hang in the triangle.

DESIGNER: BETTY BACON

Copper Pins

Pins are a great way to make a fashion statement; unique shapes add interest—wonderful projects for quick gifts—just keep a list of those who admire your pins and make duplicates for year-round gift giving.

DESIGNER: SHARON HESSOUN

MATERIALS

FOR BLACK BEAD PIN

- 25-inch (63.5 cm) length of 24-gauge copper wire
- Oval bead about 23 mm long
- 4 leaf beads 20 mm long, drilled length-wise
- 2-holed bead approximately same size as leaf beads
- ¾-inch (9 mm) pin finding

TOOLS

- Wire cutters
- Round-nose pliers
- Flat-nose pliers

MATERIALS

FOR COPPER PIN

- 12-inch (31cm) length of 20-gauge copper wire
- 6-inch length of stringing material
- 2 goldstone stars, one 3 mm and one 8 mm
- 2 goldstone hearts, one 3 mm and one 8 mm
- 2 4 mm goldstone beads
- 3 5 mm copper-colored glass beads (flying saucer shape)
- 11/0 copper-colored cut-glass seed beads
- 2 crimp beads

TOOLS

- Wire cutters
- Jig
- File or grinding tool
- Crimping pliers
- Round-nose pliers

INSTRUCTIONS

1. Cut the wire into three lengths, one measuring 6¼ inches (16 cm), one measuring 8½ inches (21.5 cm), and one measuring 10 inches (25 cm). Thread two leaf beads onto the 6¼-inch length of wire. Make a round loop at the top and push one of the beads snug against the loop. Make another loop against the bottom of the leaf bead and push the other leaf bead snug against that loop.

2. Make two loops below the second leaf bead, turning the wire in opposite directions for each loop. Thread the wire through the left side of the 2-holed bead and through the oval bead.

3. Make a spiral with four loops from the 8½-inch piece of wire. Add the other two leaf beads to the wire, allowing one of them to rest snugly against the spiral. Make a loop snug to the bottom of the leaf bead. With the top of the second leaf bead snug to that loop, make three loops below the bead, turning in opposite directions.

4. Thread the wire through the right side of the two-holed bead, pulling it down so the bottom loop is on the front of the bead, then thread the wire through the oval bead.

5. Using the two wire tails, wrap the wire around the bottom end of the pin finding to secure it in place. Wrap the 10-inch length of wire around the wires between the two-holed and oval beads.

6. Wrap the rest of the wire several times around the top of the pin finding and the two wires to secure. Be sure the ends of the wire are in the back. Tuck the ends under other wires to hide and trim if necessary. Gently bend the wires with leaves to one side to add interest.

INSTRUCTIONS

FOR COPPER PIN

1. Bend the wire around the jig pegs in an interesting, looping desingn. Work the wire around the pegs, leaving a 1/2-inch (12 mm) tail.

2. Using the round-nose pliers, bend the tail toward the back and around to form a pin catch. Bend the remaining wire toward the back and across the back to form the pin shaft. Trim off any excess length. Using the file or grinding wheel, sharpen the end of the pin.

3. Attach the stringing material to one top loop of the wire design with a crimp bead and crimp to secure. String the tail through several beads, then trim.

4. String on the seed beads and other beads, looping the stringing material through the wire design as you work. (The larger beads will help to hold the loops in place.)

5. When you are happy with the way they look, attach the other crimp bead. Wrap the stringing material around the wire design, then bring it back through the crimp bead and several beads at the end. Pull tight and crimp to secure. Trim any remaining stringing material.

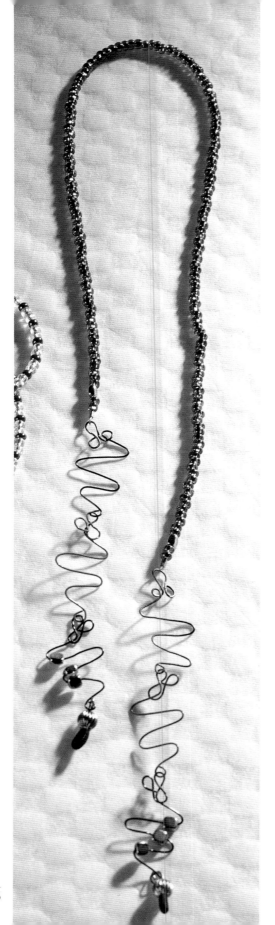

Eyeglass Leash

Here's a novel way to incorporate your favorite wire twists and beads into an everyday wearable. Be sure to use a sturdy wire and lightweight beads so the weight of your glasses won't distort your work of art.

MATERIALS

- 11-inch (28 cm) length of 22-gauge blue colored wire
- 22-inch (56 cm) length of 22-gauge green colored wire
- 8 4 mm flat square brass beads
- 2 eyeglass holder findings
- 2 tube crimp beads
- 10-12 grams of 6/0 glass seed beads
- 22-inch length of stringing material

TOOLS

- Wire cutters
- Round- or flat-nose pliers
- Jig
- Soft mallet

DESIGNER: SHARON HESSOUN

INSTRUCTIONS

1. Cut the blue wire into two 5½-inch (14 cm) lengths, then cut the green wire into four 5½-inch lengths.

2. Slide three brass beads onto one of the green wires. Set up the jig in an interesting pattern. Bend the wire around the jig, sliding the beads onto each section as you bend. Repeat with the second green wire.

3. Repeat the jig pattern with the remaining blue and green wire lengths.

4. Spread out the double-wrapped wire ends to form three circles. Harden the wire by gently pounding it with a soft mallet so it will keep its shape.

5. Attach the wire pieces together, using the photo as a guide.

6. Open the metal loop of the of the eyeglass holders slightly. Slide the metal pieces into the loop and close tightly.

7. Attach one end of the stringing material to one green wire piece, leaving at least an inch (2.5 cm) tail. Thread on a tube crimp bead, two glass beads, and a brass bead. Pull the wire tail back through all of them. Push the crimp bead up against the green wire and crimp to secure.

8. String the remaining glass beads, repeating the pattern with the brass beads and the crimp tube on the other end. Wrap and tightly crimp the other end of the strung piece on the end. Pull tight and crimp to secure. Trim any excess stringing thread..

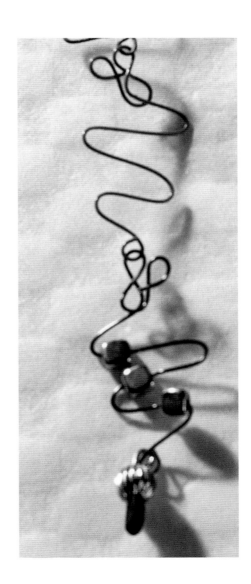

WIRE COILS EYEGLASS LEASH

MATERIALS

- 2-inch (81 cm) length of 18-gauge colored wire
- 12 grams of 6/0 glass seed beads
- Eyeglass holder findings
- 27-inch (69 cm) length of stringing thread
- 2 tube crimp beads

TOOLS

Wire cutters

Round-nose pliers

DESIGNER: SHARON HESSOUN

INSTRUCTIONS

1. Cut the wire into two 16-inch (41 cm) lengths. Wrap one of the 16-inch lengths around the round-nose pliers seven times to form a flat spiral, leaving a 1-inch (2.5 cm) tail at one end.

2. Bend the tail up flat against the spiral. Using the remainder of the wire, form a large V about 2 inches (5 cm) below the spiral.

3. Wrap the end of the wire around the tail snug against the outer edge of the spiral. Fan out the inner loops of the spiral by pushing them with your finger through the center.

4. Repeat steps 1-3 with the second wire length to make a matching piece. Don't worry about getting the spirals to be exactly the same.

5. Attach one end of the stringing material to the bottom of one V using a crimp tube. Crimp with pliers to secure. (Use a 1-inch overlap and hide it inside the beads once they're strung.)

6. String the beads on, leaving about 1 inch of stringing material unstrung. Put on the crimp tube. Wrap the end of the stringing material around the bottom of the other V, bringing it back through the crimp bead and the string beads. Crimp the tube to secure.

7. Bend the wire spiral's tail into a loop and wrap to secure. Open the loop of the eyeglass finding and slip the wire loop onto it. Close tightly. Repeat for the other side.

More Glass Bead Earrings

Glass beads make the perfect accessory for interesting bent wire shapes. Let the beads inspire you!

DESIGNER: BETTY BACON

INSTRUCTIONS

1. Cut the wire into two 4-inch (10 cm) lengths. Make a loop in the end of both wires. Three-eighths inch (10 mm) from the loop, make a soft bend in the wire opposite the loop.

2. Make a second bend ¾ inch (18 mm) from the first bend and a third bend ¾ inch from the second bend.

3. Make a loop to match the first loop ⅜ inch (9 mm) from the third bend and overlap. Place each ear wire through the overlapped loops.

4. Place a jump ring through the small bead and attach it through the bottom of the overlapped loops. The jump ring should hang freely inside the triangle.

5. Place the larger bead on a jump ring and attach it to the bottom of the triangle.

MATERIALS
- 8-inch (20 cm) length of 20-gauge sterling silver wire
- 2 small triangular and 2 medium triangular beads
- 4 jump rings
- 2 ear wires

TOOLS
- Wire cutters
- Round-nose pliers

INSTRUCTIONS

1. Cut the wire into two 4½-inch (11.5 cm) lengths. Form twists in the wire by anchoring one end of the wire in the pin vise, holding the other end with the flat nose pliers, and gently turning the pliers to achieve even spacing.

2. Make a loop in one end of each wire, letting the loop follow the natural curve of the wire. Make another loop ½ inch (13 mm) from the first, still following the curve.

3. Holding the top loop with pliers and the wire end with your fingers, make a curve about ¼ inch (6 mm) down and under the second loop, allowing the wire to follow around the outside of the loop with a gentle curve and bringing it just under the first loop, crossing between the two loops. Bring the wire down and underneath the lower end.

4. Add a bead, then use pliers to bring the wire to meet the curve on the other side. Cut excess wire. Place two small jump rings side by side on the top loop and connect with the ear wire.

MATERIALS

- 9-inch (23 cm) length of 18-gauge square silver wire
- 2 glass beads
- 4 small jump rings
- Ear wires

TOOLS

- Wire cutters
- Pin vise
- Round-nose pliers
- Flat-nose pliers
- Wire cutters

WIRE CAGE PENDANTS

Looking for a way to showcase your favorite handcrafted bead? Simply create a wire pendant for it. Designer Tip: Take care not to mar the wire with pliers as you work to prevent compromising the wire's strength.

BEAD ARTIST: DEE SNELL (LEFT) AND BRUCE ST. JOHN MAHER (RIGHT)

MATERIALS

FOR PENDANT AT LEFT

- 4-foot (3.6 m) length of 21-gauge, dead-soft, square 14K gold-filled wire
- 12-inch (30 cm) length of 18-gauge, hard, round, 14K gold-filled binding wire
- 15 to 25 mm bead with a hole large enough to accommodate four 21-gauge wires

TOOLS

- Wire cutters
- Pin vise
- Chain-nose pliers
- Round-nose pliers

DESIGNER: R.P. MYERS

MATERIALS

FOR PENDANT ON RIGHT

- 12-inch (30 cm) length of 18-gauge, dead-soft square 14K gold-filled wire
- 4-inch (10 cm) length of 18-gauge, half-hard, half-round, 14K gold-filled binding wire
- 20 to 25 mm scarab bead

TOOLS

- Wire cutters
- Pin vise
- Round-, chain, and flat-nose pliers

INSTRUCTIONS
For Pendant at Left

1. Cut the 21-gauge wire into four 12-inch lengths. Twist each of two lengths with a pin vise. Bundle the four wires together and wrap three times with 18-gauge binding wire 2 inches (5 cm) from one end. Slip the bead over the long side of the wire bundle and make three wire wraps on the other side of the bead. The bead should be able to freely rotate.

2. Separate one twisted and one untwisted wire at the bottom of the bead, holding the bead and wire bundle with the short lengths of the wire at the top. Carefully curl each of the wire bundles into a swirl in opposite directions so that the wires swing out and away from the center. Visualize an imaginary line running vertically through the middle of the bead. Pull the two wire ends together about an inch above the bead. At the point where the wires cross, form the main harness with either the twisted or untwisted wires and bend them until they are parallel to each other along the imaginary line.

3. Place the round-nose pliers perpendicular to the two parallel wires and roll the wires forward until they lie right down the center of the bead, forming the bail. Press the wires together with flat-nose pliers about ⅜ inch down from the top of the bail until the four wires are all parallel. Bend an offset hook deep enough to go over all four wires at one end of the 18-gauge wire. Wrap the half-round binding wire around all four wires, beginning at the point where the wires separate to form the bail. Crimp the ends of the binding wire so they are flat and smooth to the touch with chain-nose pliers. Cut off the excess wire about an inch below the binding and form two rosettes, referring to the photo as a guide. Separate the four wires coming out of the top of the bead and tie them off to the main harness wires as shown in the photo. Secure the tie-offs tightly but take care not to mar the wire. Spread the bail wires to the desired appearance.

INSTRUCTIONS
For Pendant at Rights

1. Twist the 12-inch length of wire with a pin vise. Find its center, move back half the distance of the bead's width, and bend the wire at just a little more than 90 degrees with round-nose pliers. Slip the bead onto the wire so that it rests against the loop, then make a second bend to match the first 1/16 inch away from the bead. Caution: Do not let the pliers come in contact with the bead to prevent chipping or breakage. Visualize an imaginary line running vertically through the middle of the bead. Pull the two wire ends together about an inch above the bead. At the point where the wires cross, form the main harness with either the twisted or untwisted wires and bend them until they are parallel to each other along the imaginary line.

2. Place the round-nose pliers perpendicular to the two parallel wires and roll the wires forward until they lie right down the center of the bead, forming the bail. Press the wires together with flat-nose pliers about ⅜ inch down from the top of the bail until the four wires are all parallel.

LILAC HYACINTH PIN

Curves and loops of wire can easily be arranged into shapes that resemble your favorite garden blooms. Use beads in the varying tones of the same color for a more realistic look.

DESIGNER: SHARON HESSOUN

MATERIALS

- 44 inches (1.12 m) 22-gauge sterling silver wire
- 27 size 6/0 seed beads
- 1-inch (2.5 cm) pin finding with holes

TOOLS

- Wire cutter
- Jig
- Round-nose pliers
- Flat- or needle-nose pliers

INSTRUCTIONS

1. Cut the wire into three 12-inch (31 cm) lengths and one 8-inch (20 cm) length. Set the jig in the pattern shown in figure 26 on page 126.

2. Slide nine beads onto a length of 12-inch wire. Find the center of the wire and move one bead to that spot. Wrap the wire around the peg at the center top to secure the bead in the loop.

3. Slide a bead on the wire as you wrap each loop, wrapping from below the peg around the top of the peg and to the next lower peg (clockwise on the right column of loops and counterclockwise on the left column loops). When you've finished, each loop should have a bead in it.

4. Repeat steps 2 and 3 with the other two 12-inch wire lengths

5. Put the three looped wire pieces together, intertwining them near the top loops. Pull the six straight wire pieces together below the loops.

6. Open the pin finding so that the pin will not be in the way as you work. Put one end of the 8-inch wire length through a hole in the pin finding. Bend the end of the wire with the flat- or needle-nose pliers to secure the wire. Wrap the wire tightly around the six straight wire pieces and the pin finding about a dozen times, ending with the wire on the back side. Trim if necessary.

7. Use round-nose pliers to bend the bottom ends of the wire in loops at random heights. Take care not to expose the pin finding when bending the wire.

(Continued from page 113)

3. Bend an offset hook deep enough to go over all four wires at one end of the half-round wire. Wrap the binding wire around all four wires, beginning at the starting point where the two wires come together from the bead. Keep wrapping until the binding reaches the point where the wires separate to form the bail. Crimp the ends of the binding wire with chain-nose pliers so that the ends are flat and smooth to the touch.

4. Hold the binding securely between your thumb and forefinger of one hand and curl the wires that lie down the center of the bead to form a swirl that nearly covers the binding wire. Sweep the remaining wires down to be tied off on one of the wires coming up from the bead. Cut the wires off about an inch beyond the point where they are to be tied off. Bend a hook at the ends of each wire and crimp them down on the main wires with chain-nose pliers. Take care not to mar the wire. Spread the bail wires to the desired appearance.

TEARDROP BEAD NECKLACE

Scroll-shaped wire links and faceted glass beads—both in contrasting sizes—combine to create a simple but stunning necklace. Note the complementary scroll design suspending the teardrop bead.

MATERIALS

- 25 mm (more or less) teardrop bead with horizontal top hole large enough for your wire to pass through
- 2 feet (1.8 m) of 18-gauge round wire
- 5½-foot (5 m) length of 20-gauge square wire
- 1 foot (31 cm) of 24-gauge square wire
- 24 assorted small- to medium-sized beads
- 22 small jump rings
- Clasp findings

TOOLS

- Wire cutters
- Pin vise
- Round-nose pliers
- Chain-nose pliers
- Flush cutters

DESIGNER: MAMI LAHER

INSTRUCTIONS

1. Cut an 8½-inch (21.5 cm) length from the 20-gauge square wire and twist it with both ends clamped between the vise. Remove the wire from the vise and cut a 4-inch (10 cm) and a 3-inch (7.5 cm) length from it.

2. Put the 3-inch length through the teardrop bead's hole and center it so that an equal amount of wire protrudes from both ends.

3. Position the 4-inch wire next to the 3-inch wire and make a hump-shaped bend in the 4-inch wire length shaped to fit over the top of the teardrop bead.

4. Cut a 1-foot (.9 m) piece of 24-gauge square wire into two 6-inch (15 cm) lengths and use them to make three or four wraps around the wires on each side of the pendant where the wires come out of the holes.

5. Bend the 4-inch wire up slightly on one side of the teardrop bead and slide a bead onto it. Make a swirl at the end of the wire to prevent the bead from sliding off. Repeat on the other side of the teardrop.

6. Bend the 3-inch wire down next to the teardrop bead and slide a bead onto it. Make a swirl at the end of the wire to prevent the bead from sliding off. Repeat on the other side of the teardrop.

7. Cut the remaining length of 20-gauge square wire in half and twist it with the ends placed in the tabletop and pin vises. Cut the twisted wire into eight lengths, each 4 inches long.

8. Using round-nose pliers, make a swirl at one end of the twisted wire, slide on one of the larger beads, and make a similar swirl at the other end. Repeat seven more times.

9. Cut the wire into 10 3-inch (7.5 cm) lengths. Make beaded swirls from these wire lengths and the smaller beads.

10. Connect the bead/swirl units together with jump rings, alternating between the twisted wire swirls and the single wire swirls. Attach the finding pieces at either end.

BRIGHT BRACELETS

Here's just an inkling of the incredible design possibilities of beads and wire. Varying the jig designs, the type of wire, and the beads can create an endless number of designs.

DESIGNER: LILLI BRENNAN

MATERIALS

FOR PURPLE BRACELET

- 16-inch (41 cm) length of 22-gauge gray wire
- 7½-inch(19 cm) length of 20-gauge silver wire
- 42 4 mm square beads
- 3 4 mm jump rings
- Clasp findings

TOOLS

- Wire cutters
- Round-nose pliers
- Jig

INSTRUCTIONS

1. Cut the gray wire into seven 2¼-inch (6 cm) lengths. Form a small loop on one end of a length of wire. Slide on three beads, then cross the wires over each other to form another loop in the center. Slide on three more beads and finish with a loop at the end. Trim off any excess wire.

2. Repeat step1 six times. Curve each wire so that the looped ends are on top of each other and shape into a circle.

3. Cut six 1¼-inch lengths from the silver wire and use the pliers to form figure-eight shapes by bending one end in a loop toward the middle from the right and the other end in a loop toward the middle from the left. Leave a small gap in the loops.

4. Attach the links by sliding the bead link loops in the figure-eight link loops. Note: One side of the bead links will have two loops (from the ends); be sure to get both loops in the figure-eight link

5. Add a jump ring to each end of the bracelet, then add the clasp findings. Tighten any loose areas with pliers.

MATERIALS

FOR BLUE BRACELET

- 19 10 mm tube beads
- 86-inch (2.2 m) length of black wire
- Clasp findings

TOOLS

- Wire cutters
- Jig
- Small nail
- Flat-nose pliers

INSTRUCTIONS

1. Cut the wire into 19 3½-inch (9 cm) lengths, two 2½-inch (6.5 cm) lengths, and one 14-inch (36 cm) length.

2. Arrange the jig according to the pattern in figure 27 on page 126. Working with a piece of 3½-inch wire, make the first two loops, then slide on a bead and finish the second two loops. Repeat with the remaing 3½-inch lengths of wire.

3. Arrange the jig according to the pattern in figure 28 on page 126 and make two links from the 2½-inch wire.

4. Wrap the 14-inch length of wire tightly arund the nail. Slide off the coil and cut down the midlle to form jump rings. (You will need 42.)

5. Assemble the bracelet by attaching the outer loops of the bead links with jump rings on both sides. Attach one link made in step 3 to each end with jump rings, then use another jump ring to attach a clasp finding to the center loops.

INSTRUCTIONS

1. Cut the wire into two 46-inch (1.2 m) lengths. Place the ends in a pin vise and twist to create the desired effect. Cut the twisted wire into seven 6½-inch (16.5 cm) lengths.

2. Arrange the jig according to the pattern in figure 29 on page 126. Place the center of the wire at the start peg and make loops 1, 2, 3, and 4. Slide beads onto each end of the wire, then make loops 5, 6, 7, and 8.

3. Attach the links together with jump rings, then add clasp findings.

POUNDED WIRE EARRINGS

Dig through your jewelry-making supplies for a few short scraps of wire and an hour later you can be wearing a pair of these great earrings.

MATERIALS

- 2 6-inch (15 cm) lengths of 16-gauge gold-filled wire
- 2 headpins
- 4 6 mm beads
- Ear wires

TOOLS

- Wire cutters
- Round-nose pliers
- Jig
- Hammer
- Anvil

DESIGNER: GARY HELWIG

INSTRUCTIONS

1. Form a loop on one end of each of the wire lengths around round-nose pliers, then bend the step of the loop in the opposite direction so that it aligns with the center of the loop.

2. Set up the jig pattern on the horizontal of the jig as shown in the illustration below. Place the wire loop end over the top peg. Wrap the wire around the pegs, then remove from the jig and manipulate the wire by hand to the desired shape. Repeat with the second wire.

3. Fold the end of each wire tail over the wire segment between the second and third pins and cut the tail to the appropriate length. Place the links on the anvil and hammer gently into the desired shape. Be especially careful not to overhammer in areas with two layers of wire.

4. Slide two beads down each headpin. Loop the top of the wire through the jig shape and wrap the wire around several times to secure. Trim off any excess wire. Repeat with the other earring.

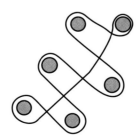

Jig Patterns

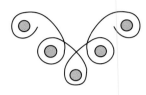

Figure 1

Figure 2

Figure 3

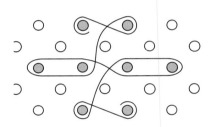

Figure 4

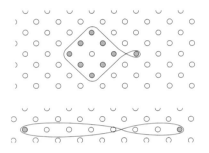

Figure 5

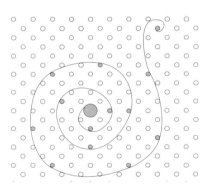

Figure 6

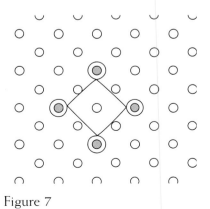

Figure 7

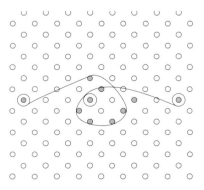

Figure 8

Figure 9

Jig Patterns

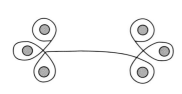

Figure 10

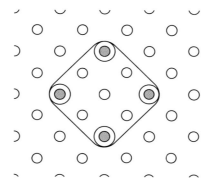

Figure 11

Figure 12

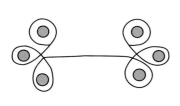

Figure 13

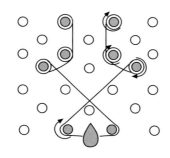

Figure 14

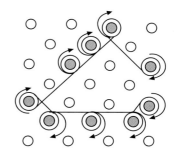

Figure 15

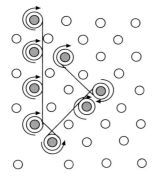

Figure 16

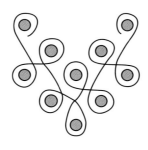

Figure 17

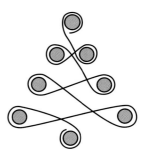

Figure 18

Jig Patterns

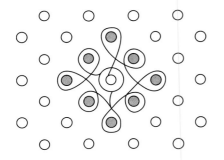

Figure 19

Figure 20

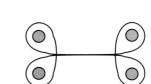

Figure 21

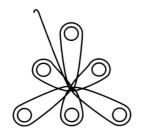

Figure 22

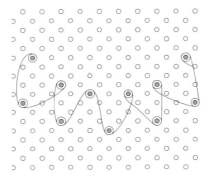

Figure 23

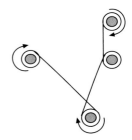

Figure 24

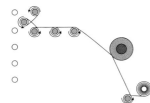

Figure 25

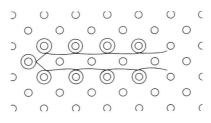

Figure 26

Figure 27

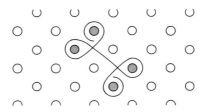

Figure 28

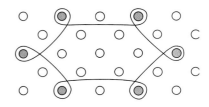

Figure 29

Contributing Designers

Dr. Carolyn Adams-Price is a psychology professor at Mississippi State University in Starkville, Mississippi. One of her main research interests is creativity and she is the author of Creativity and Aging: Empirical and Theoretical Approaches. A sampling of her jewelry designs can be seen on her website at www.capstonebeads.com.

Betty Bacon has been interested in fashion and art since childhood. She specializes in jewelry design using sterling silver or gold-filled wire combined with modern glass. She sells her jewelry through her company, Treasured Designs, in Chantilly, Virginia.

Sharon Bateman has been a freelance artist and writer for many years. She invented and manufactures Sharondipity Tube Looms, a series of amulet and bracelet looms that eliminate the need to weave in warp threads. Sharon would like to offer a special thanks to Helwig Industries, Lacy's Stiff Stuff, and Helby Imports for all their support and encouragement. She can be reached by email at sharondipity@nidlink.com

Lilli Brennan has enjoyed a lifelong passion for jewelry. After experimenting with several forms of jewelry making, Lilli has devoted her attention in the last year to various forms of wire wrapping, specializing in custom links created with the WigJig Delphi. Lilli lives with her husband and daughters in Rochelle, New York, and can be reached at lunamom@bestweb.net.

Chris Gluck is a designer living in Vermont with her two children. Since childhood she has loved all types of crafts and art. Chris' fascination with colorful plastic coated wire began when the telephone repairman left some behind! She is now an art and craft teacher and the founder of Wire Art Inc. which markets wire and kits. She can be reached by email at cgluck@together.net or on the web at www.wirearts.com.

Gary Helwig is the publisher of Wonderful, Wearable Wire and the inventor of theOriginal WigJig, Athena WigJig, WigJig Olympus, WigJig Delphi, Super Pegs, and Spiral Maker (all patent pending). He has taught and demonstrated wire working techniques throughout the country to both beginning and advanced wire workers, and is currently developing a new line of wire and bead earring designs focusing on thinner wire gauges.

Sharon Hessoun is a designer of bead and wire jewelry and accessories living in Akron, Ohio. She discovered her love for creating with beads, wire, and other metals while searching for creative ways to manage stress. Her pieces are shown at galleries and boutiques around the country and are sold at juried shows. She can be reached at shessoun@gowebway.com.

Susan Kinney is an interior designer living in Asheville, North Carolina. She specializes in both residential and commercial interior design as well as an eclectic array of jewelry, fashion items, and accessories for the home and garden. She can be reached at suezendesigns@home.com.

Mami Laher is an artist who loves more than anything searching for originality and uniqueness in the artistic form. Originally from Japan, she has lived in the United States since 1979 and currently resides in Los Angeles. Samples of her work can be viewed on her website at www.mamibeads.com.

R.P. Myers grew up in the state of Washington and has been an award-winningresidential designer for over 26 years. He is also an accomplished photographer and sculptor. R.P. took up wire wrapping five years ago to help relieve the stress of his profession. Email him at rpmyers.com/wire.

Geri Omohundro is an award-winning stained glass artist living in the Snake River Canyon of Southern Idaho. She fell in love with shaping glass in a flame during a Cindy Jenkins bead making workshop, and now creates dichroic glass beads and explores ways of showcasing them with wire-wrap techniques. Geri can be reached at www.north-rim.net/advancetogo.

Karen Ray has worked in the Navy research community for 15 years and is currently the Science and Technology Advisor to Sixth Fleet in Gaeta, Italy. In the last few years, Karen rekindled her interest in jewelry making as an artistic outlet. She says she owes all of her experience in wireworking to Marj Helwig, who always patiently inspired and encouraged her many students.

Preston Reuther is a professional wire sculptor and jewelry maker. He maintains a large website on wire jewelry making and has also produced a complete video course on the subject. Preston's on-line newsletter, The Wireworker, is available free of charge. Visit his website at www.wire-sculpture.com to subscribe.

Barbara Van Buskirk is a freelance graphic designer and bead artist. A transplanted New Yorker, she lives in Asheville, North Carolina, with her extraordinarily tolerant husband and daughter. Barbara lives by the motto "You can never have too many beads!" She can be reached by email at barbaravb@pipeline.com.

Sally Walter has a master's degree in communications from Ohio State University. She found her way to wire work via her passion for dolls—her fashion dolls needed clothing hangers and she needed a fast and fun way to create them. She found the WigJig and the result can be seen at www.thewalters.com/wire.html.

INDEX

Acknowledgements

The author would like to thank the following people
for their contributions to this book: Deborah Coule of
Chevron Trading Post & Bead Co. in Asheville, North
Carolina, for lending materials for photo shoots;
Suzanne Helwig of Helwig Industries, makers of
WigJigs (www.wigjig.com [web site] or
sales@wigjig.com [email] for her contagious enthusiasm
and for sharing her designers; and Cel Naranjo and
Dwayne Shell for the skills and laughter they brought
to photo shoots.